THREE
CATHOLIC REFORMERS

OF THE FIFTEENTH CENTURY.

by

MARY H. ALLIES.

Originally printed in

LONDON:

BURNS AND OATES.
1878.

AT THE FEET OF ST. GREGORY THE
SEVENTH,

THE PATTERN OF ALL TRUE REFORMERS,

I LAY THIS MEMORIAL OF THREE SAINTS,

WHO FOLLOWED IN THEIR DAY HIS
EXAMPLE,

RESTORING THE BEAUTY OF GOD'S
HOUSE

BY PREACHING THE PENANCE WHICH
THEY PRACTISED.

CONTENTS.

Foreword

The Fifteenth Century was a time of crisis in the Church, and therefore in Europe. The Avignon papacy had been the cause of many evils throughout most of the century preceding it, and although Pope Gregory XI returned to Rome, the next pontificate, that of Urban VI, saw a great schism rend Europe into two opposing papacies, one Roman and one in Avignon. Thus, for more than thirty years, two and even three rival popes strove to win the faithful to their allegiance, and as a result, great evils entered the Church, Conciliarism not being the least. The temporal rulers pitted pope against pope so as to win for themselves privileges advantageous to the royal power in their own realms.

Laxity was the result within the Church, for the authority that held it together was unable to rule effectively. The clergy, religious, and laity, already decimated by the Black Death, and now torn between rival claimants to the papacy, allowed themselves to sink further and further into a spirit of worldliness.

This small book contains three short biographies of three men raised up by God to help restore the Church in the late fourteenth and into the second part of the fifteenth century. The Church was in crisis, but that was hardly something new in its history. But neither was the solution very different from those former occasions. It was sanctity of life. The laxity of life, the worship of the things of this world, could only be countered and then conquered by the life of contempt for this world, and a love of Divine things. This love of God and the realities of the supernatural order filled the lives of these men here represented: Saint Vincent Ferrer, Saint Bernardine of Siena, and Saint John Capistran. The first was the great Dominican preacher of his age; the other two, sons of the poor man of Assisi, Saint Francis. All three were great preachers, all three strove to reform both Church and civil society, and all three were saints.

In every crisis, which is generally a punishment for sin and infidelity to God, the resolution to it is to be found in holiness of life, which is nothing else than the union with God through charity, as well as love of souls. This love is not the sentimental, worldly love of those whose heart seeks only to fulfil self, but the Divine love, which is poured into our hearts by the Holy Ghost. In our own time, in which the truths of the Faith and the Christian life are under attack or denied, the answer will likewise be found in sanctity. Holiness is demanded now as it was then, and holiness requires prayer and penance, contempt for the world, and union with God through Divine love. This is not a passive retreat from action, far from it. In all three of these saints, we see an apostolic fervour beyond any found in our own days. Each of these men went city by city, or realm by realm, in order to preach Jesus Christ and Him crucified, and as a consequence, the only thing important for every man that will ever live: the salvation of his soul and everlasting life.

This was the lesson of these three saints, and this is the lesson for our own times. It is to be hoped that this short introduction to their lives, will inspire

Catholics to imitate them in their desire for God and quest for their eternal salvation, and so move them to put their treasure where moth or rust can never corrupt.

Fr. Dominic Mary of the Pillar, OP
Feast of Our Lady of Ransom 2014

I.

ST. VINCENT FERRER.

1357 — 1419

CHAPTER I.

Preparation.

Towards the middle of the fourteenth century there lived at Valencia, in the Kingdom of Aragon, William, or as some say Michael, Ferrer and Constance Miguel, his wife. They were of ancient family, and having enjoyed the world in youth, they now in more mature age gave themselves up to a serious life, so that the glory of having so renowned a son as St. Vincent was not altogether undeserved. Besides the Saint they had two sons, Peter and Boniface, and two daughters, who are mentioned incidentally in Vincent's life. Boniface was a famous lawyer, but on the death of his wife he renounced the world, and exchanged his fame for the habit of St. Bruno. Both father and mother received a supernatural intimation of the greatness of the son who was to be born to them. One night in a dream Michael Ferrer thought he was in the Dominican church at Valencia, where he beheld a friar of most venerable appearance preaching. He tried hard to listen to every word of the sermon, when the friar addressing him, said, 'I congratulate thee, my well-beloved son, for in a few days thy wife shall bring forth a son whose holiness, doctrine, fame, and miraculous power shall be such that the people of France and Spain shall venerate him as one of the Apostles, and he shall be a Friar Preacher, as thou seest I am.' At these words the multitude in the church gave forth a loud acclamation, and Michael, in trying to join his voice to theirs, awoke, and aroused his wife in order to tell her in his delight of his dream. But afterwards, reflecting that they had often learned from theologians not to pay much attention to such omens, they thought but little of the vision. Two circumstances however proved to Constance that there was something unusual about the child she was going to bring forth. One was the entire absence of the physical suffering which she had experienced in other pregnancies; the other, that, strange as it may seem, she often heard a sound like the barking of a dog proceed from her womb. This last sign was interpreted as betokening the coming of a great and holy preacher, for, as the Bishop of Valencia remarked to her, a dog is a not inadequate image of a preacher. When at length Constance gave birth to her son, in the year 1357[1], people poured in to see the child of these wonderful signs, and at his baptism the concourse of curious visitors was much more considerable. Everybody seemed anxious that the child should be called after himself, till at length the priest, quite wearied out, settled the point by saying, 'Let his name be Vincent.' It was noted at the time that not one of those present nor any of his relations were called Vincent. If in God's mind the name of His chosen servants is a thing full of significance, we must see here, as at the baptism of St. John the Baptist[2], the special interposition of His will. His biographer remarks that he was called Vincent, which is from the Latin *vincere*, to conquer, 'by a kind of Divine presage,' and applies to him the passage of the Apocalypse, 'He went forth conquering and to conquer.'[3]

Only two characteristic features of his very

---

[1] The Bollandists adopt this date as the most probable.

[2] St. Luke i. 59—64.

[3] Ranzano, *Acta Sanctorum*, in die quinta Aprilis, p. 484.

early years have come down to us. He, whose preaching was to move Europe, was the quietest of children. He hardly ever cried as other babies do, but lying still, with open eyes, in his little cradle, he was delightful to behold. When he grew older, his parents helped on the perfection to which he was to attain by encouraging him in the way of virtue and moving him to become better. At nine years of age he began to show signs of that mental excellence which, associated with sanctity, is so powerful a tool in the world for doing God's work; and if he ever played with other boys, he would satisfy himself for the concession by calling them away after a very short gambol to listen to his sermon. Standing on a little eminence, he used to make them judges of his oratorical power, saying, 'Now listen to me, and tell me what sort of a preacher I shall make.' He paid great attention to the sermons he heard, whether good or indifferent, and carried away all the information he could gather from the words and gestures of the learned. Two devotions in particular were dear to his boyish heart, one which a Saint has called that of the elect, love of her who is the lily among thorns; the other, compared in Holy Scripture to the rock and the stone [4], because without it all worship of God must be feeble — devotion to the Passion of our Lord. Vincent was still in the cradle when a long drought fell upon Valencia, and its inhabitants, having vainly prayed for succour, were filled with the most gloomy forebodings. Constance's child, who had begun to lisp a few words, said to her distinctly one day, ' If you wish for rain, carry me in procession and you

---

[4] 'Mel de petra oleumque de saxo durissimo' (Deut. xxxii. 13).

will be heard.'[5] This infantine prediction was verified to the letter, and we are told that it reached the ears of Eleanor, Queen of Aragon, who begged that the little prophet might be brought to her to caress. Another instance is related of his miraculous power in boyhood; but more astonishing-still than that very power is the humility with which he exercised it. Devotion to the Passion and to our Lady would need some outward object of zeal, and if the one prompted Vincent in his childish way to labour for the souls of other boys even at his play, the other suggested to him perhaps that generosity to the bodily needs of the poor, which is a salient feature in the saints. Here again we are told of his parents that they seconded his charity, and were never vexed at his very lavish alms.[6] It is sometimes the tendency of great piety to feed, as it were, upon itself, to live perhaps too much on those devout feelings and sentiments which are a pure gift of God, and to lay but too little stress on what we might call the intellectual side of religion. It was not so with Vincent. He lived in times of strong passions which had acted somewhat like a heresy in blinding the minds of men to the Truth. His weapons were therefore twofold: there was the vocation to combat the passions, and the human learning as the natural arm against ignorance. At fourteen years of age the Saint excelled the youth of Valencia in secular as well as ecclesiastical lore, for he became proficient both in the study of theology and of philosophy, which term was applied in those days rather to logic, as the science of reasoning, than to what we

---

[5] M. L'Abbé Bayle, *Vie de St. Vincent Ferrier*, p. 5.

[6] *Vita*, p. 485.

now understand by philosophy.[7]

Vincent was seventeen when a subject of gravest interest, that of his vocation, began to occupy Michael Ferrer's mind. We venture to say that few fathers would have acted as he did under the circumstances. One day he called his son to him, and broached the important subject in words which paint conflicting emotions, the natural pride of the father who is at the same time desirous that the child of so much promise should fulfil his vocation in all perfection. 'Three things, my dear son,' he said, 'are agitating my mind and a subject of anxiety to me at this present time. If I were left to myself, I know which I should choose; but I wish first to hear your opinion, and I promise to be guided by it in this matter. I have often told you about the revelation I had concerning you from God before you were born. This and the virtues you have practised from your earliest years make me inclined to think that you should enter the Order of St. Dominic and become a great preacher of the Christian faith. Secondly, the riches which we owe to God's liberality, and the consideration of your blooming youth would induce me to seek out a fitting wife for you. Thirdly, as I perceive you have ability so great and varied that all look upon you as likely to become one of the most learned men in the world, I have been thinking of sending you either to Rome or to Paris, where your virtue and learning would come to the knowledge of the most able men, and thus you might acquire a position which would bring lasting honour on our family. These are the considerations, my dear son, which are a subject of

---

[7] Bayle, p. 11.

daily anxiety to me, but I ask you only to please yourself in your choice. Only tell me your desire, that I may comply with it whilst I can before I die.' Vincent's own mind was very clearly made up, and he replied, ' For some time past, dear father, I had been meaning to speak to you on the subject of my vocation, but as it has been God's will that you should forestall me, I will answer you in a few words and tell you all that is on my mind. The riches, pleasures, and honours of this world are most distasteful to me. Jesus Christ is the sole object of my thoughts and my actions, and so I have resolved to put on the habit of St. Dominic, and to dedicate myself to God's service in his Order. I beseech of you therefore, my dearest father, if you love me, make me worthy of your blessing, and I humbly ask the same favour of my mother, that with the goodwill of both I may set out upon God's service.'[8] It was in the year 1374. The next day, which happened to be the Feast of the Purification, the feast of all others most appropriate to a sacrifice, Vincent entered the Dominican convent at Valencia. The Superiors of St. Dominic's Order at that time did not fail to perceive the rare qualities of the young friar, whose coming had been announced to the Prior of Valencia in a dream by St. Dominic himself. They gave him ample opportunities for the full development of his mental gifts. After his profession the Fathers unanimously decreed that 'it was a shame to keep a youth of so much promise at Valencia.'[9] He was sent therefore to Barcelona, 'one of the most celebrated places,' as Ranzano quaintly says, 'which the world possesses.' Without following

---

[8] *Vita*, p. 486.

[9] *Vita*, p. 487.

Vincent to the various places whither obedience led him during the time which we look upon as that of his preparation for the apostolic ministry, we may mention that at Barcelona he gave himself up exclusively to the study of Holy Scripture, and so great was his zeal that he came to know the Bible by heart, penetrating by patient thought to the very core of its most obscure passages. He also learned Hebrew, in order to confront to some purpose the Jews who abounded at that time in Spain.

Vincent was ordained priest at the age of thirty, about the year 1388, for, according to the custom of the day, the priesthood was not conferred before the age of thirty. Two incidents in particular are related of him which belong to these years, and we put them before the reader in preference to others because they seem to give us the measure of the man. Whilst he was at Barcelona, as a very young friar and still a deacon, he began to preach, and God glorified him at the outset by allowing the grace of conversion to follow his words in a remarkable way. But He furthermore attached the gift of prophecy to Vincent's preaching. A grievous famine raged at Barcelona, and, as is so often the case, it did not come alone, but was aggravated by pestilence. Queen Eleanor by desire of the King had left the place to escape contagion. Public processions were made by the people to avert God's anger. Vincent addressed them one day in burning words, exhorting them to repent and to do penance. Suddenly he exclaimed, 'Rejoice, my brethren, towards evening two ships laden with wheat will arrive in the port, and you will be supplied according to your need.' Whilst he spoke there was a dreadful storm upon the sea, and nothing seemed more impossible than the accomplishment of his prophecy. So instead of rejoicing the people were vexed, and their discontent penetrated the walls of the Dominican convent, whereupon Friar Vincent, with all humility and calmness, received an admonition to be more prudent in weighing his words for the future. But that same evening the ships arrived, and they were the precursors of many others which shortly afterwards followed from Flanders.[10]

At a time when his mission had not formally begun, this is an example of the outward working of St. Vincent. It was already powerful, and the secret of his strength lay in the inward conviction of his nothingness, just as worldly success depends so much upon self-confidence. ' Imprint, O Lord,' cried out another Saint,[11] 'Thy Wounds upon my heart, that I may read therein sorrow and love: sorrow to endure every sorrow for Thee, love to despise every other love but Thine.' That abiding sorrow and that all-sufficient love formed the basis of Vincent's future apostolate. It is recounted of him that one day he was praying before the image of his crucified Lord, and as he contemplated the sacred Wounds, he burst out in a transport of love: 'Lord, is it possible that Thou hast suffered so much on the Cross?' And the figure of our Lord, turning its head towards the Saint, answered, 'Yes, Vincent; all this, and much more.'[12]

---

[10] M. L'Abbé Bayle, p. 26.

[11] St. Augustine.

[12] *Vie*, p. 23.

CHAPTER II.

The Apostle of the Judgment.

It would be nearly impossible to follow a Saint in spirit through his earthly pilgrimage without having before us, even if it were the offspring of imagination, some notion of the physical man. In St. Vincent's case, though we believe portraits of him to be rare, we have the description of his trustworthy biographer, Teoli. 'He was of the middle stature,' says that authority, 'well proportioned, and of beautiful countenance. His hair was golden in youth but became slightly grey in after life. His forehead was lofty and expressive of nobility and calmness. He had large brown eyes which were full of brightness and life. Modesty however was more admirably depicted there than beauty. The complexion which in youth had been so brilliant had been worn by his long mortification into an austere pallor,' and to add to this charm of his presence he had a voice which 'resounded like a silver bell.'[13] All these advantages were requisite to win the hearts of men, for to realize what those times were, it is enough to consider what is implied in an *Apostle of the Judgment.* Vincent was sent not to one nation or people in particular, but as if all the countries of Europe had been found wanting in the spiritual measure, his apostolic working extended itself to Italy, France, England, Ireland and Scotland, and this ministry of preaching did not end with him, but was continued up to the year 1456, when St. John Capistran, his second successor, and the Apostle of Peace, was

---

[13] Quoted by M. l'Abbé Bayle, p. 84.

called to receive the crown.

Vincent was labouring in Castille in 1390 when the famous Peter de Luna came to Spain as Legate of the Antipope, Clement VII, in order to secure that country's allegiance to his master's cause. Peter, who had the merit of recognizing Vincent's virtues, wished to carry him off to Avignon, but the Saint refused, thinking he could work more powerfully for souls where he was. We shall see later that this meeting with the future Benedict XIII. influenced the whole of his subsequent career. For the time he developed a particular power for the conversion of the Jews, which no doubt helped to prepare men's minds for his future announcement of the Judgment. At Valladolid a learned Rabbi, who heard the Saint's forcible preaching, honestly owned that although the ancient Law was his one study, the new preacher understood it far better than he did, and he embraced Christianity, to become, later, Bishop of Carthagena.

When Vincent returned to Valencia, he was appointed confessor to the Queen of Aragon, wife of John I. He had some difficulty in managing his royal penitent, who was by no means devoid of feminine curiosity. Having begged to be allowed to see the Saint's cell, a request which he pointedly refused, the Queen took it upon herself to gratify her wish. Vincent was in prayer before the Crucifix, but he was invisible to the Queen. The religious who was with her begged him to notice her entrance, and to greet her, but he firmly replied, 'Are you not aware that our cells are closed to women? The Queen is here in spite of my prohibition. She will see me only when she consents to leave my cell.' No sooner had the royal culprit repassed the threshold of the cell than her confessor again became visible to her. His face expressed the strongest disapproval. ' Your Majesty's fault would have cost you dear,' he said to his disobedient penitent, 'if ignorance and a want of reflection did not in part excuse it. In future take care not to repeat your act, for God would severely punish you.'[14]

At this time of Vincent's life, before he left for Avignon, we place three particular and significant temptations which may be taken to represent the fire whereby he was salted.[15] As before the work of the Ministry our Lord was led into the desert to be tempted by the devil, so His servant Vincent was tried and perfected by assaults of the same nature. One night as the Saint had finished reciting his Matins before a statue of our Lady, and was praying earnestly for the grace of final perseverance, the devil under the form of an old man of most majestic figure appeared to him, and addressed him in these words: 'I am one of those ancient hermits who inhabited an Egyptian solitude for many years in great continency and rigorous fast from meat and drink. When I was young, I gave myself up to every sensual pleasure, but afterwards, when I had spent my youth in various delights, I came to myself, and did penance, and thus our most merciful God pardoned me my sins. Now therefore, if thou wilt listen to me, who have so much experience, I should persuade thee to have mercy

---

[14] *Vie de St. Vincent Ferrier*, p. 53.

[15] 'Omnis enim igne salietur' (St. Mark ix. 48).

23

on thy flourishing youth, to spare thy bodily mortifications now, and to reserve them for thy old age. For doubt not that God is always ready to accept the repentance of sinners.' When the Saint had first beheld the solitary, he was seized with fear, but afterwards he perceived the venom of these words, and suspected his visitor to be the devil. Signing himself with the Cross he made answer: 'Begone, thou pestilent serpent, for by thy cunning words thou hast proved thyself not one of the hermits of Egypt but one of the devils of Hell. Thou didst think to overcome the new soldier of Christ with thy snares; but although I am new in this warfare, the grace of Christ, for Whose love I have encountered temptations and labours, makes me so thoroughly armed that I do not fear to fight thee.' The devil hearing this retort vanished with a howl, leaving a fetid smell in the cell. 'Command that these stones be made bread,'[16] he had said to the Master. To the disciple it was: 'Spare thy youth.'

Another night Vincent was praying before a crucifix when the devil again appeared to him, this time in the form of a huge blackamoor, threatening him and saying: 'I will pervert those prayers and works whereby thou thinkest to gain Heaven until I cause thee weakly to succumb.' And the holy soldier of Christ answered: 'As long as I have the grace of Christ, no one of thy threats shall terrify me.' 'Nothing,' replied the devil, 'is more difficult than perseverance in that grace of which thou speakest.' 'He,' rejoined Vincent, 'Who enabled me to begin will enable me also to persevere.' Thus the second great temptation was overcome. It was like the word

---

[16] St. Matt. iv. 3.

spoken to our Lord by the same seducer of men: 'If Thou be the Son of God, cast Thyself down.'[17]

For the third assault we can find no parallel in the case of our Lord. The bitterest hatred has spared the purity of the Virgin Son where it has not always rendered justice to the Virgin Mother. Once towards the fourth hour of the night as Vincent was reading St. Jerome's treatise on the perpetual virginity of our Blessed Lady, and praying that he, too, might preserve fidelity to the same holy state, he heard, as if in answer to his thought, a voice say: 'We cannot all be virgins, and although thou hast kept thy virginity up to this hour, I will no longer suffer thee to enjoy this privilege.' At these words the Saint was filled with trouble and sadness, and kneeling to invoke the Mother of fair love whom he had always cherished, he begged that she would tell him their meaning. After a while he was rewarded with a vision of our Lady, who comforted him, saying: 'The words which thou hast just heard were spoken by the devil, who puts before thee the difficulty of goodness in order to deter thee from any longer pursuing virtue. But do thou only be cautious and thou shalt persevere. For although the devil will lay many snares for thee, and strive to endanger thy virginity, be not discouraged. Hope in God, He will be the shield whereby thou shalt not only easily despise the devil's weapons, but overcome him and his artifices.' [18] Vincent possessed, as we have seen, great personal attractions which served to facilitate the work of the powers of darkness. A certain woman at Valencia

---

[17] St. Matt. iv. 6.

[18] *Vita*, p. 487.

fell in love with him, and feigned illness in order to manifest her passion to the holy friar. He took refuge in flight, and when the woman, like Putiphar's wife, began to accuse him of seducing her, she became suddenly possessed by the devil, who through the mouth of the miserable creature, rendered testimony to Vincent's virtue, 'You shall not expel me from this body,' he cried out, 'unless that man comes back, who, placed in the midst of the fire, preserved himself unscathed from the flames.' [19] On another occasion his enemies, probably those who were jealous of his sanctity, bribed a bad woman to occupy his cell, and put her there one evening whilst the Saint was still at his devotions in the church. When Vincent saw the woman, he took her for Satan, as well he might, and addressed her as a 'cursed devil.' But instead of being seduced, it was Vincent who brought her then and there to penance, and shortly afterwards she married in order to lead a new life. The artifice practised by a false brother at Valencia, a friar preacher whose immorality had often called forth Vincent's reproaches, presented a still more diabolical character. The calumny was laid bare, and the Saint's pardon readily given to the inventor.[20] So the words of our Lady announcing 'many snares' soon began to be accomplished.

In 1390, as we have seen, Peter de Luna, the Pope of Avignon's Papal Legate, had come to Spain to plead his master's cause. What that cause was, or rather what claim Clement VII. could allege to be

---

[19] *Vita*, p. 489.
[20] *Vita*, p. 490.

called the Successor of St. Peter, rests entirely upon the Conclave which elected Urban VI in 1378. Never perhaps was there a stormier election. Even before Gregory XI died, secret meetings were held in Rome to secure an Italian as his successor, and whilst the Cardinals were sitting in Conclave, the populace wildly vociferated: 'We want a Roman or an Italian.' The Sacred College, composed of twenty-three members, [21] numbered eighteen Frenchmen, who probably understood the Roman temperament very ill. The only way to oppose expressed wishes would have been to act with the same prudent hesitation as is customary on these occasions. But the Cardinals took fright, and although the Conclave had promised to be long, they speedily elected the Archbishop of Bari, Bartolomeo de Prignano, who assumed the name of Urban VI. All historians seem to agree that this Pontiff loved justice too rigorously, and that he was too much bent upon sudden reforms. Now three-fourths of his Cardinals were French *grands seigneurs*, who probably had the faults of their class. Pomp and splendour were their natural surroundings, and when, regretfully indeed, they followed Gregory XI to Rome, they had exchanged luxury and a respected Papacy at Avignon for a city torn by factions, and a life, if we may so speak, from hand to mouth. Yet there was a deep justice in that wild outcry of the Roman people. Beneath its impatient vociferations we can read this meaning: 'It is wiser for the Pope to lack ease and perhaps personal safety in Italy than for the Papacy to be absent from its lawful seat.' During three months after his

---

[21] Hergenrother, *Kirchengeschichte*, vol. ii. erste Abtheilung, P. 34.

election the Cardinals acknowledged Urban VI as the true Successor of St. Peter. Then they could bear with his rough goodness and his efforts at sweeping reforms no longer. Urban was abandoned by eleven French Cardinals and Peter de Luna, who declared the Holy See vacant.[22] Let us suppose he had shown a different and a more conciliating spirit during his administration, no one would then have attempted to doubt his election. Here lies, as it seems to us, all the point of the question. The residence at Avignon had tended to nationalize the Papacy, which by its very nature is placed above nationality, as the power which makes all nations one house of Christ. As a consequence of that false position, which had lasted from 1305 to 1377, Frenchmen now made the schism, and continued on the race of Avignonese rulers by the election in 1378 of Robert of Geneva. When he came to die in 1394, the Spaniard, Peter de Luna, was chosen by the French Cardinals, and he took the title of Benedict XIII. Whilst we render homage to the ability of his personal character, we might fitly liken him to the man spoken of by our Lord who 'answering said: I go, Sir, and he went not.'[23] His time was passed in summoning consultations as to how the schism could be extinguished, whilst that most, desirable effect lay in his own hands, and he constantly refused to speak the one word which would have brought it about. Vincent's holiness had, however, made an indelible impression upon the Legate, as Benedict XIII fully proved. When in 1396 he lost his Carmelite confessor, who was nominated to a bishopric in Catalonia, he sent for

---

[22] Bruck, *Kirchengeschichle*, p. 425.

[23]

the Saint to make Vincent his spiritual guide. There was worldly wisdom, too, in the choice, for the sanctity and presence of Vincent at his Court would throw a sort of spiritual lustre over that Court itself. If such a thought crossed Benedict's mind, as it probably did, history has proved the justness of his calculation, for if there is an advantage to be met with on the side of the Antipope, it is in the supposed adhesion of St. Vincent Ferrer to his cause. We say *supposed*, because obedience to the lawful Successor of St. Peter or to the Antipope at Avignon was not a personal matter or choice. England, Germany, Denmark, Switzerland, and Poland sided with Urban, whilst France, Aragon, Castille, Scotland, and Portugal acknowledged Peter de Luna. Acceptance or rejection of the lawful Pope was a national question, and thus St. Vincent's side was found for him. We know that he used in vain all his influence with Benedict to persuade him to resign 'for the peace of the Church.' In those days it was far more difficult than it is in these times of easy communication to get to the bottom of a vexed question, and if Benedict spoke of 'peace when there was no peace,' the case was far otherwise with Vincent. At the brilliant Court of Avignon the Saint practised his rule with the utmost fidelity, and although the position was extremely distasteful to him, he bore with his repugnance out of deference to Benedict's command. But God had other designs with regard to His faithful servant: 'I came,' our Lord said, 'to cast fire on the earth, and what will I but that it be enkindled?' All His saints feed their desires upon the same holy flame.

The Church was Vincent's dearest thought, and therefore one wish was uppermost in his heart, the desire to restore its outward unity under one head, whom all nations should unanimously acknowledge. We have seen that they who made the schism could allege no formal obstacle against Urban's election. On the contrary, they acted as they did out of a motive of personal disaffection to him. He might have been injudicious, but how weak must the principle of monarchy have become in a country where so slight a cause leads to deposition of its prince! The extraordinary perversity shown by the cardinals who receded from Urban was another result of Avignon, and is important to note. As then the Saint, in great trouble of mind, was pondering how he could remedy a state of things which caused many souls to perish, he felt suddenly seized with fever. For twelve days he lay dangerously ill, and at the last his sickness seemed to be fatal. Whilst he appeared to be dying, his eyes were opened, and he beheld our Lord shining upon him with great brightness. A multitude of angels and the Patriarchs, St. Dominic and St. Francis, accompanied their Lord, and comforted the Saint in what seemed his apparent extremity. Then our Lord spoke these words: 'Be constant, O my servant Vincent, and put away all trouble from thy mind. For as I have already made thee strong in many temptations, and have delivered thee from many snares of both men and demons, so for the future and unto the end My grace shall accompany thee. Now I will deliver thee from this bodily sickness and this mental anguish, for peace shall soon be restored to the Church. As soon as thou art cured, leave the Court of Benedict, because I have chosen thee as a special preacher of My Gospel. My command is that in humility and poverty thou shouldst traverse the lands of France and Spain to evangelize them. After thy words and works have borne plentiful fruits, thou thyself shalt die at the ends of the earth.[24] But amongst other things pertaining to thy preaching, thou shalt announce to the people the near approach of the Day of Judgment, correcting them without fear of their crimes. And although thou wilt suffer many calumnies at the mouths of wicked men, fear not, because I shall be with thee always, and under My protection thou shalt avoid all dangers, and easily despise the wiles of thine adversaries.'[25] When He had spoken these words, our Lord touched Vincent on the cheek, and after giving him further instruction for his future ministry, disappeared.

In this vision our Lord bestowed two things on his servant Vincent. The gift of health was the first, for He is one who never asks impossibilities, and always enables His creatures to do His will. He had told a dying man to teach His Gospel, but one touch of that Divine hand brought Vincent back from the valley of the shadow of death. His second gift was a definite purpose and object, for the vision determined the whole of Vincent's subsequent career. This may be said to have taken a new development in obedience to the special prescription which our Lord had deigned to give by the extraordinary favour of a personal appearance.

Thus Vincent rose in health and strength from his sick bed when the vision had departed, and the next day he visited the astonished Benedict, who had despaired of his life. It was in vain that the Saint solicited leave to begin his ministry as the

---

[24] Finisterre (?).

[25] Vita, p. 491.

Apostle of the Judgment. Benedict required the support of his services and disinterestedness far too much at that time to listen favourably to the proposition. Early in 1398, the French King, Charles VI, joined his instances to Vincent's, and together they urged Benedict to resign his position for the good of the Church. Then seeing that nothing could be gained from one whose words alone were so fair, Vincent left the Papal Palace for a house of his Order at Avignon. Certain prelates of Benedict's Court gave the colouring of their own minds to this act, and represented to their master that Vincent's services had been inadequately rewarded. Benedict listened to the suggestion, called a consistory, and offered the Cardinal's hat to the Saint. But the desire for apostolic labours, not the wish for greater honours, had prompted Vincent to the step, and as he refused the Sacred Purple, he said to Benedict: 'I am too much honoured already by the charge of Master of the Palace and that of confessor to your Holiness, but I must carry out God's commands to preach the Judgment to all nations.' We can judge of the anguish of his apostolic spirit during the time at Avignon, when, raised from a dying bed in a miraculous way, he was still fettered in his zeal by his deference to Benedict's wish. The state of things which called for his ardent voice and burning example can be no better described than by using his own words: 'I think there has never been so much vain luxury and impurity as there is now in the world, for we should have to go back to the Flood in order to find worse times. Bad women fill the inns and country places, and the number of them is so great that they infect the world, and will infect it still more. It is impossible to prevent the bad fruit from tainting the good when both are mixed. What dreadful avariciousness we see, what usury disguised under the pretence of certain contracts! With priests it is the reign of simony, and with religious that of envy. The intemperance of laymen and of priests is such that the fast of Lent, the Ember Days and vigils, are no longer observed. Anger is so common that amongst those who pretend to be friends murder is not infrequent. Indeed, vice is so far in the ascendant, that individuals who prefer prayer and the service of God to the world and its pomps are called useless and idle.'[26]

One day, when Vincent was weeping over the delay which Benedict's refusal put upon his work, a voice seemed to come from the crucifix, saying, 'Go, I will wait for thee still.'[27] The Saint's prayers and tears were soon to fructify.

CHAPTER III.

Preaching with Authority.

When at length Benedict suffered the Saint to depart, Vincent was in the full vigour of his manhood. At forty-one the illusions of youth are gone, if not its fire and spirit, but it is one of the properties of sanctity not to grow old, that is to say, to keep freshness of heart amidst the increasing shadows of advancing years. This feature was remarkable in St. Vincent.

---

[26] *Vie de S. Vincent*, p. 65.
[27] *Vie*, p. 65.

Instead of following him in this chapter to the countries which occupied his zeal for the last twenty years of his life, we may attach ourselves more particularly to the description of what that life was, and to the nature of the ministry which he undertook in obedience to the Divine commands at Avignon. Amongst all the servants of God St. Vincent Ferrer is one of those who deserve in a special manner to be considered as representative saints, therefore the mode of his ministry cannot fail to have an importance of its own.

Benedict XIII, then, blessed the undertaking which he would no longer prevent, and gave to Vincent the faculties of a Papal Legate. In the year 1398 he set out thus fortified for Spain. His native land received some of the first fruits of his labours, for on his way thither, as though he could brook no further delay, his hunger and thirst for souls took an active form. His eloquence was already prodigious, and in Catalonia the people began to follow him from place to place. The mode of his reception in a town was one which would have upset an ordinary man's self-command. The clergy in their vestments, the magistrates in their official robes, besides the nobility of the place, came out to receive him 'as if he had been one of God's Apostles.'[28] *Non nobis, Domine, non nobis, sed Nomini Tuo da gloriam*, cried out the object of these royal honours. The Saint tried, however, to stay the fervour of these outward demonstrations except when he saw that they were conducive to the good of souls. A wooden barrier was invented to preserve him from the multitudes

---

[28] *Vita*, p. 495.

who pressed upon his steps, and would inevitably have crushed him in the helplessness engendered by a crowd. Vincent's manner of evangelizing a country was most complete, for he went through it, stopping at the smallest places, according to the need of souls. Before entering a town he fell on his knees with all his band, and with tears and sighs he besought the Divine inspiration for the people to whom he came. The faculties conferred upon him by Benedict XIII were renewed by Martin V, the Pontiff duly elected at Constance, but in spite of his full powers Vincent never failed to ask the leave and the blessing of the local authority wherever he happened to be preaching. As long as he could he travelled about on foot, till in his latter years a wound in his leg obliged him to ride. Then he used the humble ministry of an ass, wishing in all things to. preserve the voluntary poverty of his state. *Non nobis, Domine, non nobis, sed Nomini Tuo da gloriam.* He was truly preaching in the Name of God, and so vividly was the fact impressed on the minds of those to whom he went that trade stopped in a measure in places which listened to the Apostle. The universities were closed, artisans and merchants left their commerce to sit at his feet; in short, his voice carried with it an irresistible invitation to attend to the one thing necessary. Churches and public places were too small to contain his audience. His improvised pulpit was ordinarily raised in an open space which opposed no limits to the crowd. Towards the end of the fourteenth century ecclesiastical preaching had become infected with a touch of Pagan reminiscences, the consequence of a period of transition from scholastic learning to humanistic studies.

Vincent's method adopted a truer bent. 'Jesus Christ,' he said, 'did not command us to preach Ovid, or Horace, or Virgil, but the Gospel.' And he enlarges on the subject in a sermon on the parable of the Sower. 'Human life is preserved by the seed which is sown. To preach is to sow the seed of wheat of the New Testament in the field of consciences. It is this which preserves the spiritual life and the Catholic faith. . . . The Bible is the seed of Jesus Christ which produces devotion, charity, penance, salvation; cockle must be kept carefully away from these fruits, and the cockle may be represented by quotations from heathen poets. The Apostle St. Paul preached for the space of thirty-seven years, and we do not read that he quoted the poets more than three times.'[29]

Once when he was asked whence he drew the beautiful thoughts of his sermons, he answered, pointing to a crucifix, 'There is the book where I learn all that I preach, there it is that I study my sermons.'[30] His preaching was founded upon a long and fervent meditation of the Holy Scriptures at the feet of Jesus crucified, but as true devotion to our Lord's Passion produces fear of the Lord, it is recounted of Vincent that when he spoke of the Judgment, the terror which his vehemence caused amongst the people was such, that falling upon their knees, they would cry for mercy. His own life was a daily wonder even in that age, when, if sensuality was as rife as in our times, great mortifications were frequent too. Vincent's sleep lasted five hours, and and he took this repose either on the ground or on a

---

[29] *Vie*, p. 88.

[30] *Vie de St. Vincent Ferrier*, p. 86.

bundle of rods, spending the rest of the night in prayer and the meditation of his beloved Bible. At midnight he always rose to say Matins on his knees, finding great devotion in weighing every word of the Divine Office. Early in the morning his laborious day began. Every morning he who was to be the apostle of reconciliation for so many souls humbled himself first in confession. He then sung Mass with a devotion so full of unction that his tears fell plentifully from the Canon to the Communion. Afterwards he put on the habit of the Friar Preachers, and began his sermon, uttering those words which the Holy Spirit put into his mouth. Sometimes it lasted two or three hours, but so far from causing fatigue to the multitude, they may be said to have hung upon his lips. Then he heard the confessions of those who were determined to reform their lives, and at midday he took his single meal.

It is impossible to become holy without a certain amount at least of bodily mortification, but, as it may be surmised, Vincent was an expert in this art of the saints. Except on Sundays, his life was a continual fast, and every evening he took a rigorous discipline, unless he was ill, when he caused it to be given to him by one of his companions. The remainder of the day was spent in again hearing confessions, in preaching, and in the effort to consummate by his private influence what he had begun in public, for he went about to inns and frequented places, seeking to reconcile enemies, to bring about the restitution of ill-gotten goods, and to console weary hearts. But if by the rigour of his life and the favourite theme of his preaching, 'Do penance, for the Kingdom of God is at hand,'[31] he was like that Precursor of our Lord who laboured to eclipse himself for the expected Messias, there is one very striking point of resemblance between Vincent and his Divine Master. During the time of the Ministry we read of three classes of men who hung upon His words as He passed from place to place. There were the chosen twelve Apostles, the disciples, and the mass of the people. So in this respect our Lord allowed Vincent to be like Himself, for three corresponding classes of men appeared at the preaching of this apostolical Saint. He had twelve companions, who answered to the College of Apostles, and were more intimately connected with his labours, as they helped him in the distribution of the Sacraments and his spiritual works of mercy, and belonged moreover to the Dominican Order. Besides these Fathers, other secular priests joined St. Vincent's company, and the second class consisted of them and of other persons of the world who wished for a life of greater perfection. The women were separated from the men, and married people could not become members of this kind of confraternity unless they separated by mutual consent. But the Disciplinists formed the most striking feature of the assembly of disciples. With that utter disregard of human respect, which was so often noticeable in the Middle Ages, these people followed Vincent to do public penance for their crimes. Every evening, according to his institution, each one of them bared his shoulders for a self-inflicted discipline, whilst he repeated the formula:

---

[31] 'And John came into all the country about the Jordan, preaching the baptism of penance for the remission of sins ' (St. Luke iii. 3).

'May this be unto the memory of the Passion of Jesus Christ and for the remission of my sins.'[32] As in the teaching of our Lord, the third class of auditors was the mass of the people. The sincerity of the Disciplinists was so great that they moved to contrition those who beheld them at their penance. A characteristic of St. Vincent is recorded with regard to them. Once at Lyons, a soldier, who was a great sinner, confessed to one of Vincent's priests and received for his penance to take part in the evening procession of the Disciplinists and in their discipline. The soldier strongly objecting, the confessor referred the case to Vincent, who said, 'Tell your penitent merely to go to the procession, and not to take the discipline.' But the effect of those strokes and tears on the soldier was such that he caused himself to be well disciplined of his own accord. On arriving in a new place the Saint was accustomed to recommend his company to universal hospitality. The injunction was hardly needed, for in those days charity towards those who came in the name of God was regarded as a duty. When however we are told that his company sometimes numbered over ten thousand,[33] such courtesy did indeed amount to a great virtue. The pilgrims wore a dress of sober colour significative of their life; the men walked on foot preceded by a crucifix, whilst a banner of our Lady was carried before the women. In our days penance would not probably take the form of following a preacher even if he were a saint. The words of a St. Vincent Ferrer might produce some remarkable vocations, a greater frequentation of the Sacraments, or perhaps

---

[32] *Vita*, p. 494.
[33] *Vita*, p. 494.

a rigorous temperance movement, but it must not be forgotten that Vincent's mission was directed against the causes in the Church which had produced the schism, or rather suffered God to allow it. Thus very possibly the only efficacious way of acting upon the masses was adopted by the Saint. After him in the toils of his ministry followed other living instances of the power of penance, and of the thirst after greater perfection. Considering that idleness and neglect of the sacraments are the roots of so much evil in the Church, Vincent stipulated that each member of his company should not only sell all his goods on entering it, but also continue to exercise his profession and to gain his livelihood by labour. They received the sacraments at least once a week, which was often for those times. Vincent clearly expressed what was expected of his followers when he said once, speaking from the pulpit: 'We admit no one among us without first putting him through a strict examination to get to his true intention, and to judge what profit he can gain from this change of life. If he has a wife and children we do not want him![34] He must be resolved to do penance, and not be merely bent upon going from one country to another, nor upon eating and drinking without solicitude!' Vincent, it will be observed, had the merit of saying exactly what he meant, or rather, of freely giving speech to a disagreeable truth, and he used the same liberty of language when it was necessary to bring the great ones of the earth to their senses, taking no account of persons, but thinking only of immortal souls. The maxim of St. Augustine, 'Love the man while you hate his errors,' should be the basis of all dealings

---

[34] Except under the condition already mentioned.

40

with vice and infidelity. Speaking once to the inhabitants of Chinchilla, he exhorted them to the best proof of penance, perseverance in goodness. 'Good people,' he said, 'many of you have entered on the right road; you have done penance, you have accomplished some good works, you have taken the discipline, you have put on sack-cloth; you have fasted, you have heard sermons and Holy Mass, you have been to confession. The governors of the town have taken effective measures for the prevention of crime and public sins, but I beg of you, persevere. Do not let it be said of you, "One day they keep the commandments, another day they break them." This is what we have to deplore in certain towns, which, I fear very much, will imitate Ninive. The Ninivites did penance on account of Jonas' preaching, but persevered not.'[35] As if Vincent had been a type of the great Judge at the day of wrath, his very countenance when he spoke of the judgment struck terror into the hearts of sinners. Putting aside all human respect, it often happened that before a multitude of people they would kneel at the Saint's feet and make public confession, but when they had done what was in their power, Vincent never failed to show them the sweetness of true sanctity.[36]

He possessed too what, to say the very least, may be looked upon as a wonderful grace of converting the Jews, since the number estimated to have become Christians by his ministry is said to be twenty-five thousand. Once when the Saint was preaching at Ezija in Spain, a Jewess of great wealth

---

[35] *Vie de St. Vincent Ferrier*, p. 101.
[36] *Vita*, p. 494.

and influence in the place was amongst the audience. She was so obstinate in maintaining her errors that she did not welcome the light of the true faith which came to her from Vincent's words. As he spoke on, she silently tried to find an objection, yet as if the Saint read the secret struggle, as fast as she did this, he refuted her in his sermon, just as though he had been preaching for her sole benefit. At last she could bear it no longer, and moved to leave the church, but the congregation knowing her well, and hoping for good results if she would only listen, opposed her departure. Vincent seeing what passed, addressed these words from the pulpit, 'I beg of you to let her go, but at the same time I ask those persons who are sitting under the porch to move their places.' The invitation was obeyed, but the Jewess had no sooner reached it when it gave way, burying her under a heap of stones. The poor creature was of course dead. The Saint brought her back to life in the name of Jesus of Nazareth, and her first words were, 'The Christian religion is the true one, and there is no salvation out of it.'[37] This wonderful conversion seems to belong more especially to the class of graces which are bestowed as much for the souls of others as for the individual in whose favour they work.

'These signs,' our Lord says, 'shall follow them that believe: In My Name they shall cast out devils, they shall speak with new tongues, they shall take up serpents, and if they shall drink any deadly thing, it shall not hurt them; they shall lay their hands upon the sick, and they shall recover.'[38]

---

[37] *Vie*, p. 149.
[38] St. Mark xvi. 17, 18.

These words of our Lord are fully borne out in the life of His servant. It is related of Vincent that the gift of tongues was given to him like unto "one of the Apostles," and this assertion is fully proved by the fact that in all the countries which he visited, he spoke nothing but the dialect of Valencia, for the ancient language of Castille was adopted much later as the language of Spain.[39] The power of making himself thus understood was far more extraordinary then than it would be even now when with fewer dialects there is a much greater zest for the cultivation of foreign languages. Moreover the Saint's audience, however widely dispersed, heard him equally well, and often in the course of his sermon it happened that he was obliged to pause in order to give free course to the tears and sighs of the multitude. Each day the sick were brought to him that he might lay his hands upon them and cure them in the 'Name of the Lord Jesus,' if such were God's good pleasure. Towards evening the Saint ordered one of his company to ring the *Miracle Bell*, and at its sound, they who had need of the physician either came or were brought to the church. Vincent made use of this formula in curing corporal diseases, 'These are the signs which shall follow those who believe: they shall lay their hands upon the sick and the sick shall be cured. May Jesus, the Son of Mary, the Lord and Salvation of the world, Who brought thee to the Catholic faith, preserve thee in that faith, make thee blessed, and deliver thee from this infirmity.' These words are perhaps a paraphrase of the Psalmist's, *Audi filia et vide* — 'Keep the faith and be thou cured.' The Saint does not say, *Be thou cured*

---

[39] Under Ferdinand and Isabella.

and keep the faith. Sometimes Vincent would answer the request to work more wonders by the confession that the power had gone out of him. 'I have worked miracles enough today. Do you what they ask. God Who operated through me will make use of you too to show forth His glory.'[40] Vincent then could transmit to another the empire over sick human nature which he possessed so plentifully by God's grace. The Prior of Lerida asked him once to visit a pious lady who had been a great benefactress to the Order, and was dangerously ill. 'Father Prior,' answered Vincent, 'you wish me to go and cure her by a miracle. Why cannot you work this miracle? Go, I give you my power, not only for this sick lady but also for all those whom you may meet on your way.' And the Father going forth cured five sufferers on the road before reaching the pious lady, whom he likewise restored to health as Vincent's deputy. The Saint was once preaching in Catalonia in a place called Villa-Longa, and there followed him a multitude of six thousand people. Certainly the man who undertook to provide food for so many deserved a reward, and so thought Vincent. His name was Justus, and he had placed wine to be served in a portable cask. When the people had refreshed themselves, Justus found his portatoria still quite full of wine, and wondering how this could be, he told the Saint, who made answer, 'Go and give thanks to God. They who practise works of charity deserve to see miracles of this kind. But I exhort you to remember the grace, and to keep the wine which has been thus multiplied in order to give it freely away to all who ask it of you.' For the space of ten years during which time this miraculous wine lasted,

---

[40] *Vie*, p. 81.

it cured the infirmities of those who drank of it. A woman came to the Saint's feet shedding many tears, holding in her arms a child who had been dead twelve hours. Vincent, considering that her faith was great, answered her tearful supplication by saying, 'Go to thy house and persevere in giving praise to God. This child now sleeps but it shall awake after thou hast entered thy house.' She believed and her child awoke from the sleep of death according to the Saint's word. At another time as Vincent was preaching at Valencia, a dumb woman was brought to him by a believing crowd. 'What wilt thou have, daughter?' he asked her when he had raised his eyes to Heaven. The dumb woman recovered her speech momentarily to answer, 'I wish for bread and my speech.'

'Thou shalt have thy daily bread as long as thou livest,' he said, 'but thou canst not obtain thy speech, for in view of thy future good God has been pleased to deprive thee of it. *For if thou hadst the power of speaking, thy sharpness of tongue would lose thee thy soul and thy body.* But do not cease to praise God in thy mind, and be careful not to ask Him in future for that which He has denied thee with good cause.' When the woman had answered, 'Holy Father, I will do as thou sayest,' she fell back into her former state of dumbness. [41] What a moral this scene contains, for was it not as great a miracle in the spiritual order to make a dumb woman accept her dumbness with perfect resignation as it would be to give her speech in the natural order? We must not omit one other instance of the Saint's healing power, because it is so characteristic of him.

---

[41] *Vita*, p. 503.

In Galicia, a man totally blind came to ask for his sight. 'No,' answered Vincent, 'I cannot work this miracle. Whence dost thou come?'

'From Oviedo,' replied the suppliant.

'Then return thither. Go to the Cathedral, kneel down before the crucifix, and tell our Lord that I send thee to Him in order that He may cure thee.' The blind man obeyed and received his sight.

The power of working miracles does not always suppose the knowledge of hidden and future events, but it is certain that St. Vincent possessed the gift of prophecy in a remarkable degree. He often learned by revelation what was passing in other places, or it might be in his own presence where his bodily eye could not reach. Once, for instance, as he was preaching to a great multitude at Toulouse, some of the people climbed the surrounding walls in order to be able to hear him. Amongst them was a young man, who, sitting behind the Saint, could not possibly be seen by him. The youth began to grow sleepy, a very dangerous occupation in so perilous a position. Suddenly Vincent stopped his sermon and exclaimed, 'There is a youth behind me who is sleeping on the wall, and who, if somebody does not rouse him, will fall, to the eternal perdition of his soul. Therefore make haste to help him, and deliver him from so great an evil.[42] Not amongst the minor graces of this great Saint must be reckoned his peculiar power of persuasion as exerted on Jews. One day he was about to begin his sermon as usual, but he made so

---

[42] *Vita*, p. 501.

long a pause that the people wondered what it could mean. 'Do not be astonished,' he said, 'this is the reason of my silence. I am waiting for the grace of God, which will soon be sent from on high, for you will see a concourse of men at this sermon whose coming will fill us with gladness. Use therefore all possible courtesy with them, that they may find their places ready prepared.' The Saint had hardly finished speaking, when a multitude of Jews appeared, and said they had come by a sudden inspiration of grace.[43] We will cite two remarkable instances of his prophetical power. At Barcelona, a mother brought him her child, who was suffering from a severe rupture. The Saint, inspired by the Holy Spirit, exclaimed, 'Rejoice, my daughter, and hope in the Lord, for this child shall speedily be cured of this infirmity, and when he grows up, he will become a priest, and later, a most renowned theologian.' Signing the infant with the cross, according to his custom, the infirmity immediately disappeared, and in course of time his words received their full accomplishment. Still more striking was Vincent's announcement to Francina Borgia, mother of the future Callistus III. One day, seven months before her son was born, he met Francina in the course of his peregrinations. 'You bear a child,' he said to her, 'who will become Pope;' and later on, when her son was born, 'Take care of this little child, for he will become Pope and canonize me.' Some years afterwards, Alfonso Borgia went as a student to hear Vincent preach, and being much impressed with his words, observed to him, 'You preach wonderfully well; you will be a saint.' ' And you will canonize me,' answered

---

[43] *Vita*, p. 501.

Vincent.[44]

'In My name they shall cast out devils.' In the dominion over the powers of evil lies one of the highest tests of sanctity, for as our Lord said in designating one of the legion, 'This kind is only cast out by prayer and fasting,'[45] by those, that is to say, who have conquered the concupiscence of the flesh. A daughter of a certain man at Valencia had been troubled many years by the evil spirit. Eight men hardly sufficed to carry her to the Saint, in whose presence she became so terrible to behold that she herself appeared to be rather a demon than a human being. Vincent reduced her to silence by these words: 'I command thee on the part of Jesus Christ to restrain thyself, and to desist from this violence.' Then questioning the evil spirit within the unfortunate girl as to the causes of the possession, he received this reply: 'Seven years ago, I with some of my companions entered the house of her parents in the middle of the night for the purpose of persuading the husband to murder his wife. But it fell out far otherwise to what we had hoped, nor could we succeed in our endeavour. For the wife, alarmed by the noise we made, awoke, and armed herself with the sign of the Cross, invoking the names of Jesus and of His Mother, Whom we fear so much, as thou knowest. We, seeing that she had recourse to arms so powerful, shook the whole house in great indignation. This girl, who was then ten years old, fearing lest the house should fall, hid herself under the bed for, as she thought, greater security. But I would not go away without doing

---

44 *Vie*, p. 333.
45 St. Mark ix. 28.

some mischief, and seeing that I could not hurt the husband or wife, who had crossed themselves, I took possession of this girl, who had not crossed herself, and I have remained up to this present time, vexing her more or less as it pleased myself.' When the Saint had commanded the devil to go out, he retorted: 'Many before thee have conjured me to leave this body, but they had not sufficient power to compel me. But thou art called Vincent; thou hast conquered me, and I am not able to resist thee. Behold I am ready to obey thy command.' On another occasion the devil entered a man during Vincent's sermon, causing him to behave like a madman, first dancing and singing,' then alternately laughing and weeping. The Saint imposed silence till the end of his discourse, and when he questioned the devil as to his reason for coming there, received this significant reply: 'This man had supported a bad woman in her vice, and because after listening to thy exhortations, she had given up this poor wretch in order to do penance, he hates thee and those who follow thee, and speaks much evil of thee. Today he came to the sermon, not indeed that his soul might profit, but in order to catch thee in thy speech. Therefore allow me to torment him until I shall have sufficiently revenged thee.' And the Saint, whose power was thus acknowledged by Satan, replied: 'I am a servant of Jesus Christ, Who prayed for His executioners, therefore in His name I tell thee to leave the body of this sinner.' When upon this formal command the evil spirit had departed, the unfortunate man was unconscious, but Vincent wished the cure to be entire, and he charged one of his priests to wait for returning life by his side.[46]

---

[46] *Vita*, p. 505.

Another time the devil owned to Vincent that he afflicted a certain man with possession because 'he ate and drank without saying his grace, or even making the sign of the Cross.'[47] Ranzano estimates at seventy the whole number of possessed cured by the Saint.

These signs and wonders testify to the greatness of inward grace in the soul of St. Vincent. Five powers of the wonder-worker were his in all their plenitude — the gift of tongues, the knowledge of hidden and secret things, the curing of sickness, raising of the dead, and dominion over the devil. He seemed to draw men after him in the odour of his ointments, for of many places, if not of all, which listened to his ardent words, it might be said as it was of Toulouse, 'The inhabitants were reformed by the miracles, words, and more especially the example of the apostolic man.' [48] To preserve humility of heart in the midst of the honours which were so generally bestowed upon St. Vincent as an outward confirmation of his mission, was in itself a miracle of grace. On the occasion of his last visit to Valencia, a Franciscan Father, who witnessed the almost royal welcome shown to the Apostle, asked him in a low tone, 'Father, what does vanity make of it?' 'My friend,' answered Vincent, ' it comes and goes, but by God's grace it does not remain.'[49] It happened once that the Saint was suffering from a loss of voice, which prevented him from preaching for some days. ' God willed it,' he said later, to prevent me from becoming vain-glorious on

---

[47] *Vie*, p. 127.

[48] *Vie*, p. 127.

[49] Ibid. p. 229.

account of my numerous sermons, and to remind me that He could take away my voice for ever.'

Those only preserve humility of heart in the enjoyment of ineffable graces who never forget that they are channels ever flowing from the great ocean of God. '*Non nobis, Domine, non nobis*', repeated Vincent in the strength of this conviction; '*sed Nomini Tuo da gloriam*'.

CHAPTER IV.

The Angel of the Apocalypse[50]

The life exemplified in the last chapter extended itself over twenty years. So far we have attached ourselves rather to the mode, now we will consider the place and time of Vincent's ministry. His itinerary in its broad outlines is thus specified by the Bollandists in their Preface to the life by Ranzano. In 1398 he evangelized Avignon and its neighbourhood; 1399, Catalonia; 1400, Provence; 1401, Piedmont and Lombardy; 1402, Dauphine; 1403, Lombardy and Savoy; 1404, Lorraine; 1405, Genoa, Belgium, Flanders; 1406-7, England, Ireland, and Scotland; 1408, various parts of France, Granada, and Alexandria in Italy; 1409, Spain; 1410, Florence, Pisa, Siena, and Lucca; 141 1, Spain; 141 4, Majorca; 1416, Constance; 1417 — 1419, Brittany.

It will be seen that the Saint's working

---

[50] Apoc. xiv. 6, 7.

affected three countries in particular, viz., France, Spain, and Italy. Of these three, two acknowledged the Avignonese Pope, whilst the third rendered allegiance to the lawful Successor of St. Peter. If any think that this was rather in virtue of its birthright than from a meritorious discrimination, yet Italy has ever been the country of sound traditions.

Vincent then departed from Avignon in 1399 and journeyed on foot to Catalonia, where he publicly unfurled the banner of penance. On his way he inaugurated what was to become a custom with him, by evangelizing or at least preaching in, the various places where he was obliged to stay. At Graus he established the Confraternity of Disciplinists, whose acts were a paraphrase of the Miserere. Nothing was heard at the evening meeting of the members but the stroke of the discipline, interrupted sometimes by plaintive cries such as: 'Mercy, Oh my God!' 'Jesus, have mercy on me.' As a remembrance of himself, Vincent left a crucifix to the town of Graus at his departure. In each place he lodged at a monastery of his own Order, or in default of that, at some religious house. His steps were directed by no other motive than the good of souls, which gives his wanderings an outward want of method. Already in 1400 he left his fruitful working in Spain for the newer battlefield of Provence. The particulars given by his biographers about his mission there are useful in conveying to us a notion of the amount of time ordinarily spent at a place by the apostle. It bears witness to the fact that his apparent want of method was in reality due to his more than human knowledge of spiritual needs. Thus he was at Aix from the 27th of October, 1400, to the 1st of December, and again on the 5th of

January, 1401, for five or six days. Seven years later he visited the place once more, staying there one single day.[51] The greatest success recorded of the Saint in these parts was the transformation of a certain valley popularly called Vallis-puta on account of its crimes. Four classes of sin in particular made it deserving of its name, for, says Ranzano, immorality, thieving, the practice of magical arts, and murder, were necessary qualifications in order to live there unmolested.[52] This barbarous people had opposed every endeavour to draw them out of the abyss of their crimes, for they had put some missioners to death and frightened away others. The knowledge of their misery and wickedness was a bait too tempting for Vincent's zeal and self-sacrifice to be set aside. Accompanied by his penitential company he went forth against them in the spirit of his motto, *Non nobis, Domine, non nobis, sed Nomini Tuo da gloriam.* In a few days he touched those depraved hearts, and by a true baptism of regeneration the Vallis-puta came to be christened Vallis-pura, a name which it bore up to the time of Louis XI. In 1401 Lombardy and Piedmont solicited the grace of the Saint's presence. We find him passing a month at Genoa, and answering the request to obtain the discharge of a criminal, sentenced to death for his grievous crimes, by these words: 'Far be it from me to disturb the course of justice, or to prevent the just punishment of criminals. All that I can do will be to beg that he may die by a less painful death.'[53]

---

[51] Vie, p. 121.
[52] Vita, p. 497.
[53] Vie, p. 128.

The Saint's own account of his labours at this time is preserved in a letter to his General dated from Geneva, and which we would place in the year 1403, for although his itinerary marks Lombardy and Savoy at this date, still in a life of so active a ministry, only the broad outline of his movements can be given. Amongst other things he says: (and it must be remembered how much St. Vincent's sermons differed in point of length from those to which we are now accustomed), 'I have often been obliged to preach two and three times a day, and besides that to sing solemn Mass. Travelling, eating my meal, sleeping, and other exercises leave me hardly a minute to myself I am obliged to prepare my sermons on the way. At the request of a number of people I went to Lombardy, where, during the space of a year and a month, I preached continually in all the cities, villages, and towns of both obediences. In the countries beyond the Alps I found many valleys where heretics, chiefly Vaudois or Cathari, abounded, and this was more especially the case in the diocese of Turin, which I traversed. I visited these valleys with method, preaching Catholic truth in each, and attacking errors. *I remarked that the principal cause of heresy was the lack of preaching.* For thirty years all that they had had in this way was from certain Vaudois heretics, who went to them twice a year from Apulea. From this, Most Reverend Father, I realize the sin of bishops and others, who, in virtue of their profession and ministry should preach to the people, and who prefer rather to stay in large towns and to amuse themselves in elegant rooms. But the souls whom Jesus Christ wished to save by His Death, these souls are perishing for want of priests. There is nobody to give bread to these children; the harvest is plentiful, but the labourers are few.'[54]

The years 1404 and 1405 were spent by Vincent in unwearied labours at Lausanne and Lyons, and in Lorraine and Flanders. His mode of life was always the same; and there is no record anywhere of that which, according to our modern notions, should be one of the ingredients of labour, rest and recreation. On the contrary, the mere act of getting from one place to another, especially in those times, implied an amount of fatigue which gradually wears out the powers of the brain. Vincent accomplished all his travelling on foot up to the year 1408, when his ardent and laborious search for souls had produced a sore in his leg which rendered much walking impossible.

Genoa remembered the Saint with gratitude as a true apostle of peace, and when Benedict XIII visited the place in 1405, he wished for the company of his former confessor. Vincent, as we know from the testimony of ancient documents, improved the occasion of this his second visit to evangelize the environs of Genoa, but perhaps he made it his primary object during his sojourn there to use strong arguments with Benedict as to the desirability of a resignation. He did not fear to tell his former penitent that, "at the tribunal of Jesus Christ, all the evils of the Church would be laid to the charge of him who believed himself to be its head, if he did not cause those evils to cease in renouncing the Papacy, whatever his right to it might be, because the extinction of the schism depended upon this renunciation. The flock is not

_____

[54] Vie, p. 135.

for the pastor, but the pastor is for the flock. If he has the charity of Jesus Christ, he ought to be ready to give his life for his sheep. What sort of crime does he commit if he quietly sees them perish? and what will his punishment be if, in order to keep a phantom of greatness for himself, he himself is the cause or means of their perdition."[55]

We have now reached an epoch of Vincent's ministry which would be full of interest for Englishmen, did we but possess more complete information as to what he effected in this country. In the summer of 1406 our King, Henry IV, sent a ship to St. Sebastian, which was to bring the Apostle to England, but details are wholly wanting. He foretold to Henry IV certain events which were to come to pass after his death, possibly the Wars of the Roses and the misfortunes of the House of Lancaster; but on the whole, perhaps, it is not a consoling fact that Vincent passed more than a year in the British Isles. As we have seen that he stayed in a place for a long or short time, according to the needs of souls, we must conclude that he found much spiritual good to do. As Henry IV had received him with almost royal honours, so, later on in 141 7, when the Saint was preaching in Normandy, at that time the domain of the English King, Henry V showed the same appreciation of sanctity. At the head of the nobility he welcomed Vincent at the gates of the town. He witnessed a miraculous cure, and heard the burning words of the Saint in a sermon on the text, *Ego resuscitabo eum in novissimo die*; but, to prove what we have said, Vincent could not be persuaded to stay more than

---

[55] *Vie*, p. 145.

three days at Caen.[56] Compared to the good of souls, the entreaties of royalty had small weight. The years 1408 and 1409 were passed by Vincent in France and Spain, and it was towards the end of 1408 that he received what to him no doubt was a most consoling invitation to the last Mahometan stronghold in Spain. The King of Granada, Mahomet Abenbalva, attracted by his fame, was curious to hear the great preacher about whom every one was talking, and he sent to fetch him, giving him at the same time leave to propagate the Gospel in Granada. All seemed to promise well: the Saint preached three sermons, which proved only too successful. The Alfaquins, so the Moorish priests were called, took fright, and although a considerable number of Mussulmen had been converted, and Abenbalva had resolved to receive Baptism, they put the resolution of the King to a trial which it was far to weak too resist, being stronger in their false religion than he in his search for truth.[57] They told Abenbalva that if he became a Christian, they would no longer acknowledge him, and he, placed between two royalties, chose that of time, freely renouncing the precious inheritance of the faith. Calling Vincent, he begged him to depart quietly, otherwise he would expose himself to violent measures.[58] The Saint left the Moorish domain with a sorrowful heart. At Guadalascara he protested against the bad habit of swearing which prevailed there, and this gave rise to the popular proverb, 'Let all be content with saying yes, like

---

[56] *Vie*, p. 319.

[57] St. John xix. 15.

[58] *Vie*, p. 147.

Friar Vincent.'[59] But even Friar Vincent knew what it was to preach in vain. At a certain place called Cuenca, where the inhabitants were leading most immoral lives, the bad women were so enraged against the Saint, that they obliged him to take to flight. It was at Gerona, in 1409, that Vincent worked a most stupendous miracle in favour of unprotected virtue. A man who wished to leave his wife, and could find nothing against her, because she was most virtuous, had recourse to calumny. A few months previously she had borne him a son, whose birth the father had pretended to attribute to adultery. The poor mother was almost heart-broken, but the holy preacher consoled her by telling her to come to his next sermon with the baby of eight months old, and to beg her husband to be present in the congregation. She came, and at the end of the discourse, Vincent, speaking to the child, said, 'Leave your mother's arms and seek out your father amongst the crowd who are here to listen to me.' The baby obeyed, and going straight up to his father, took him by the hand, exclaiming, 'This is my father. I am really his child.'[60] The man was so overcome by the wonder, that it worked a complete change in his life.

National as well as private enmities called for the Saint's arbitration, and when by the death of the King of Aragon the crown was disputed, the succession of the nearest blood relation, Don Ferdinand, was chiefly due to him. The political weight attached to Vincent's counsels is a striking

---

[59] Digan todos seguramente, Asi lo dice Fray Vincente.— Quoted by M. V Abbé Bayle.
[60] *Vie*, p. 166.

feature in his career, for is it not one of the highest proofs of sanctity to be cherished by the great, and still to love the little ones of the earth? The Saint visited Majorca in September, 141 4, staying till the 23rd of February following, during which time he reaped a plentiful harvest for the faith amongst the Moors. A very humorous anecdote is related of him whilst there. A tavern keeper came to beg the support of his preaching on the duty of paying debts, for the man had sold some wine on credit and could not get his money. 'Very good,' answered the Saint, 'I shall say how guilty those people are who keep their neighbour's goods. But I should like to know what sort of wine it is that you sell.'

The publican fetched a bottle, saying, 'Taste and see how good it is.'

'Pour some of it on my scapular.'

'But I - shall spoil it,' replied the man, perhaps in some trepidation.

'That is my affair. Do as I tell you.'

To the publican's great astonishment the bottle produced wine and water: the wine fell on to the ground, whilst the water remained on the scapular. Then Vincent remonstrated strongly with the man for his unjust adulteration, and the publican, touched with contrition, made good his cheating, and entered the Saint's company.[61] Had St. Vincent lived in these days would he not have required to perform this miracle more than once?

---

[61] *Vie*, p. 237.

We have now briefly considered his action in the order of time up to the Council of Constance in 1414, which will belong to the next chapter.

Two places in particular seem to have shone like bright stars of virtue under the Saint's influence — Valencia and Toulouse. Sanctity does not banish national feelings or love towards a native place, it idealizes them, and makes nationality into a true and particular devotion towards the souls of fellow-countrymen. How often in the lives of the Saints is not this purified love traceable in their actions, or even prominent in the hour of death. Vincent fully acquitted himself of his natural debt to Valencia. An ancient document says that 'it has become an earthly paradise. People might almost think that Almighty God wishes to re-establish here the state of original justice and innocence which our first parents lost for our greater misfortune. Every man keeps a pure heart in his mortal flesh, a pure soul, an unsullied conscience, he goes before his Creator in a state of perfect innocence, desiring nothing but Heaven.'[62] The mission at Toulouse in 1416 lasted only one month, but produced fruits which did not die for many long years. The town literally poured itself out to listen to the Saint. Trade stopped for the time, and one thought occupied men's minds almost exclusively, that of their eternal salvation. When, on Palm Sunday, Vincent took for his text, *Surgite, mortui, et venite ad judicium*, he inspired that fear of God which is the beginning of wisdom. In this instance the people in the church are said to have fallen on their knees, and waited for his reassuring

---

[62] *Vie*, p. 232.

comfort before they would rise. In the following year, at the Carnival, the inhabitants of Toulouse exchanged the noisy mirth which generally signalizes this season abroad for processions of penitents, who bore a crucifix and at the same time did public penance, as St. Vincent had taught them, for their former dissoluteness.

If in humility of heart St. Vincent had predicted his own canonization, so one day in the same spirit he proclaimed himself to the people of Salamanca as the Angel of the Apocalypse. Both announcements rested upon the petition expressed in the words, *Non nobis, Domine, non nobis, sed Nomini Tuo da gloriam.* 'What, O Lord, if I should be a saint or even an angel to exalt Thy Name?'

He was speaking of the angel seen in the Apocalypse, who said to all the nations of the earth, 'Fear God, and honour Him, because the hour of the Judgment is at hand.' 'I am that angel,' added the Saint. At these words a murmur was raised in the congregation, as if Vincent had spoken with presumption. He observed it, and wishing to confirm his assertion by a sign, as the apostle of One Who can cause weak things to confound the strong, he said, 'Have patience, and be not scandalized at my words. You shall soon clearly see whether or not I am the Angel of the Apocalypse. Go to St. Paul's Gate. There you will find a dead woman. Bring her here. I will raise her to life to prove the truth of what I have been saying.' The woman was found just in time, as they were carrying her out to burial, and brought to him. In the midst of a dead silence, the Saint addressed her, 'Woman, in the name of God I command thee to arise.' And she who had been dead immediately rose to her feet. 'Now that thou canst speak, say whether or not I am the Angel of the Apocalypse who was to preach the Judgment to all men.' 'Yes, Father,' cried out this witness from beyond the tomb, 'yes, you are that angel.'

'And now,' pursued the Saint, 'wilt thou die or live,' and upon the woman's reply that she would willingly live, Vincent answered, 'Live then.' Her course was prolonged for many years, during which time she bore witness to her resurrection from the dead.'[63]

The reason of this marvellous power we have in the holy Gospel. 'If any man minister to Me,' our Lord says, ' him will My Father honour.'[64]

CHAPTER V.

The Harvest.

We have seen that St. Vincent belonged to the obedience of Benedict XIII by the very fact of his being a Spaniard, but that he never ceased to labour for the unity of the Church, and that he witnessed with intense sorrow the conduct of the man to whom nevertheless he owed so much. Proceeding upon the view that Vincent's mission to preach penance was given to him by God in order to bring about a true and Catholic reformation for the destruction of the schism, we shall see now in

---

[63] *Vie*, p. 206.
[64] St. John xii. 26.

the closing stage of his life whether his labours were in vain. The vision of our Lord at Avignon pointed to this moral renovation, for it was as though He had said to St. Vincent: 'If men wish to see the end of the schism, let them do penance.' How grievously the want of unity impeded the full action of the Church is gathered from the testimony of the University of Paris, which was surely no partial authority concerning the Holy See. A deputation of its Doctors waited upon Charles VI in 1393 to prove to him that if 'the fair beauty of the Church were dishonoured, if the world set upon a dangerous incline was dragged down to evil and had thus put aside all respect for God and man, it was due to the schism.'[65] In 1409 the Conventicle of Pisa augmented existing evils by the election of a third Pope, so that Benedict XIII, the offspring of the first schism, was reigning at Perpignan, Gregory XII the successor of the lawful Pope, Urban VI, at Gaeta, whilst Alexander V, elected by the Cardinals of both obediences at Pisa, took up his abode at Bologna.[66] Vincent's mission of penance had at that time still five years to work before the desired effect could be obtained. Ninive had indeed begun to turn from its sins, but Ninive was not yet converted.

The Saint was the oracle and the soul of the Conferences which were held at Narbonne and Perpignan in 1415, and attended by the Emperor Sigismund, the King and Queen of Aragon, and various other ambassadors and legates from the Council of Constance which had opened in 1414. The sermons which he preached to these great ones

---

[65] *Histoire de la Papauté pendant Le XIVe. Siécle*, tom. iii. p. 132.
[66] Brück, Kirchengeschichte.

of the earth still turned upon his favourite theme:
'Do penance, for the Kingdom of God is at hand.'
The resignation of John XXIII. and of Gregory XII
brought out the obstinacy of Benedict XIII in its
true colours. If any man had ever believed in his
sincerity or in his devotion to the interests of the
Church, such credulity was no longer possible. The
Conferences of Narbonne decided that it must be
one of two things: the abdication of Benedict XIII,
or the refusal of the Kingdoms of Spain to recognize
Peter de Luna's claims. Whilst the determined old
man couched his obduracy in the humblest
language, telling the Emperor Sigismund that 'for
the service of God he would give up everything,'
Vincent used his final arguments to conquer so
selfish an opposition. The voice which had cast out
devils and called the dead back to life was, however,
impotent to remove the moral impediment of
obstinacy. But the Fathers at Constance would
brook no further delay. Peter de Luna was formally
deposed, and Vincent himself published the decree
in his country of Aragon in January, 1416,[67] thus by
one of his last public acts removing the support of
his name and sanctity from the Antipope's cause,
and preparing the way for the acceptance of
Cardinal Otho Colonna, who was elected by the
Council of Constance in November, 1417, and took
the name of Martin V. By this decision the nineteen
years of Vincent's arduous ministry were happily
crowned by the prospect of peace for the Church.
Just as dangerous illness is not cured at once, but is
so often followed by tedious convalescence, so the
Schism of the West was not instantaneously killed
by the decision of Constance. A mere phantom of

---

[67] Hergenrother, Kirchengeschlchte, ii. p. 84.

an Antipope existed up to 1429 at Peñiscola, near Valencia. Peter de Luna and Muñoz, his successor, were used as a tool by the King of Aragon, who, wishing to intimidate Martin V, and to obtain the investiture of Naples, played a very dangerous game with the expiring schism. But Vincent's labours bore their fruit in the true instincts of the people of Aragon, whose sympathies never belonged to the intruder at Peñiscola. At length, in 1429, Muñoz willingly laid down his arms, renouncing the Pontifical insignia. The schism was starved out, and the peace of the Church happily consummated.

But now toil and austerity had worn out Vincent's, physical powers, and as he turned his steps to the 'extreme west,' where the vision had foretold him that his last resting-place should be, his body was so broken that his untiring zeal for the conversion of souls presented an almost miraculous character. In 1417 Brittany received the Apostle of the Judgment and the last fruits of his ministry, as if to prove that if the schism had been brought about by Frenchmen, Frenchmen for that very reason needed the last accents of his unwearied exhortations to penance. If, says his biographer, he made places where he stayed but a few days like 'temples of religion,' eradicating every species of vice and setting up virtue, what must he have done for Brittany where he spent two years? [68] His weakness was so great that he could hardly walk without support, and speaking had become a difficulty, yet directly he ascended the pulpit, his ardour was precisely the same as in the zenith of his life and strength. He took pleasure, too, in calling to

---

[68] *Vita,* p. 509.

him little children, as if in his last days he wished more particularly to resemble those whom our Lord commended in the words, 'Of such is the Kingdom of Heaven.'[69] The Saint taught them to say the 'Our Father,' the 'Hail Mary,' and 'Apostles Creed,' and to make the holy sign of the Cross.[70] His blessing obtained the grace of fruitfulness for the Duchess of Brittany, whose marriage had previously been sterile, and it was at Vannes that he cured a paralytic who had been suffering for eighteen years, with the words: 'Silver and gold I have not, but I pray the Lord Jesus Christ in His immense charity to grant thee the health which thou askest.'

After two years had passed, the companions of the Saint pressed him, as he was already old and worn out, to return to his own country that he might die in his native land. When he thought of the prediction at Avignon, 'Thou shalt finally die at the ends of the earth,' Vincent constantly opposed them. But if the prediction applied to Brittany, his Fathers remonstrated, it seemed no less suited to Spain. At length the Saint was prevailed upon to depart, and exhorting the inhabitants of Vannes to continue in the fear of God, he set out on his ass with his companions in the middle of the night. But at dawn when they ought to have been many miles away from Vannes, they found themselves before its gates. Vincent saw in this a confirmation of his presentiment, and returning, said: 'My brethren, let us go back into the city, for we cannot alter the fact that it is God's will I should give up my spirit into His hands in this city.'

---

[69] St. Mark x. 14.

[70] *Vita*, p. 509.

'Blessed is he who comes to us in the name of the Lord,' was the greeting of the women and children, who came forth to kiss his hands, whilst Vincent told them, 'his children,' as he called them, that he was come back to them not to preach but to die. The next day he was taken ill, and having predicted the time of his death, he sent for his confessor, and received the last sacraments with great devotion.

When it became known in Vannes that the Saint was lying on his death-bed, the Bishop, magistrates, and nobility set out simultaneously to bid him farewell. Vincent's words have been preserved. He reminded them in what a state of vice he had found their country on coming to it, and that there was nothing he could have done for the salvation of their souls which he had not done. 'It remains to you,' he said, 'to persevere in the same path of virtue, and to be mindful of what I have told you. For seeing that it is God's will my life should end in this city, I will be your patron before His tribunal, and will constantly pray for you if you are faithful to my recommendations. Farewell, in ten days God will call me hence.'[71]

Considering the contention which might arise later respecting the Saint's body, they who were in authority in Vannes resolved to ask him his own wish. He answered: 'I am a religious, a poor man, and a servant of Christ, therefore I have my soul's salvation at heart, not the care of my body. I ask you to allow the Prior of the nearest monastery

---

[71] *Vita*, p. 509.

of Friar Preachers to undertake my burial.'

When nine days had passed, knowing by revelation that his end was very near, he begged, like our own Bede, to have the Passion of our Lord according to the four Evangelists read to him. Then it seemed as if he had a foretaste of the eternal joy to which he was hastening, for his countenance became radiant. Murmuring the words: *In manus tuas, Domine, commendo spiritum meum*, he entered into the bosom of God. It was the 5th of April, 1419. The Saint was therefore sixty-two years of age. At the time of his death a multitude of white butterflies were seen flying into the room. They hovered over the holy corpse, then vanished, filling the air with a most sweet fragrance.

The See of St. Peter is the centre of all Catholic hearts. The great idea embodied by the Saint, who in evangelical poverty, chastity, and obedience, departed to eternal rest on that April day was this: If vice had made the creation of an Antipope possible, virtue could and did dethrone him. Even within the Infallible Church of Christ there is but one remedy for human corruption: the generous purification of the human heart and will.

II.

ST. BERNARDINE OF SIENA.

CHAPTER VI.

A Prophet with the Mantle of Elias.

There was more than an ordinary connection between St. Vincent Ferrer and the Saint who shares with St. Catherine the patronage of the city of Siena. In 1408,[72] that is in the tenth year of his own ministry, when the great Spanish Apostle was preaching at Alexandria in Lombardy, he foretold that his mantle should descend upon one who was then listening to him, and he bequeathed to this Eliseus those parts of Italy which his ardent voice was not to reach. 'Know, my children,' these were the words of his prophetical spirit, 'that there is amongst you a religious of St. Francis, who will shortly become famous throughout Italy. His doctrine and example will produce great fruit in the Christian people. And although he is young and I am old, a time will nevertheless come when the Roman Church will exalt him in preference to me. I therefore exhort you to return thanks to God, and to ask Him to fulfil what He has revealed to me for the good of the Christian people. Because of this future ministry, I shall return to preach in Spain and France, and bequeath to him the evangelizing of the remaining peoples of Italy which I cannot undertake.'[73]

The successor thus formally designated by St. Vincent was Bernardine of Siena, one of those chosen souls who from their youth upwards have

---

[72] We adopt this date as the most probable. Bernardine was then a very young friar, as he made his profession in 1403.

[73] *Ex Analectis* dc S. Bernardino Senensi.

borne the sweet yoke of Jesus Christ in perfect innocence of mind and heart. If in other lives women have proved a snare and a temptation, they had a special mission to the childhood of one whom God had chosen for so important an inheritance. Their piety indeed sheds an aroma over Bernardine's early years which prepares us for the future triumphs of his sanctity. Is it not true to say that the pure of heart are endowed by God with singular strength for coping with sin and vice, or that purity is in itself the most powerful weapon against all that is not pure? For in its Christian meaning it is no negative or passive virtue, but one, which even in the holiest life is acquired, if we may so speak, at the point of the sword.

Bernardine's parents, called Tollo and Nera Dini, were both noble; his father belonged to the ancient family of the Albiceschi, and was a citizen of Siena, whilst his mother was a native of Massa. Tollo had received a most honourable mission from the Sienese Republic, that of Governor of Massa, a town situated at about thirty miles from Siena. It was there that Nera gave birth to Bernardine on the 8th of September, 1380. The little child, who came into the world upon the same day as our Blessed Lady, did not long enjoy the protecting arms of his parents. Nera was called away in 1383, and three years later Tollo followed his young wife of twenty-two to Heaven. At six consequently Bernardine was an orphan, and from that time a succession of holy women supplied the place of his natural guardians, and guarded all his steps with that calm watchfulness which is peculiar to holiness. His Aunt Diana was the first of the number, and for the space of five years Bernardine remained at Massa under her protection. What that protection was is exemplified in her great solicitude as to the kind of society with which her little nephew should mix. She would often say to him: 'You will learn goodness with the good, but the unjust will turn you away from God,'[74] and true to this maxim, she would suffer him to frequent only those places which offered no temptation to his eyes or ears. Purity and charity are sister virtues. One day when Diana had barely sufficient bread as a provision for her household, she refused a poor man who came to beg for food. 'Pray, pray,' said little Bernardine, 'do not send him away, and I promise you to go without my supper to-night to make up for it.'[75] Of this Saint, as of St. Vincent, we are told that from the early years of his boyhood he excelled, in letters, and that he had a fondness for preaching the sermons which he had heard to other boys. When he was only eleven his Aunt Diana died, and Bernardine was adopted by Cristoforo and Pia, his wife, who belonged to the Albiceschi family, and lived at Siena. Up to that time his studies had principally consisted in grammar; a wide term in those days, but on his arrival at Siena, he made the acquaintance of a famous master, John of Spoleto, who besides being a great professor of philosophy, was renowned for his goodness. When Bernardine had made steady progress in secular learning under John's guidance, he gave himself up to the study of canon law and that of the Holy Scriptures, and compared to the others this latter science seemed to

---

[74] *II. Vita a Maphaeo Vegio Laudensi*, p. 750. *Acta Sanctorum, in die Vigesima*.

[75] *II. Vita a Maphaeo Vegio Laudensi*, p. 750. *Acta Sanctorum, in die Vigesima*.

him the one thing necessary.

He spent three years on his religious education, and all that time Pia followed in the footsteps of his Aunt Diana, watching over him to keep off the faintest breath of evil. His companions well knew with whom they had to deal, for the announcement 'Here comes Bernardine'[76] would act as a complete check upon unguarded conversation.[77]

To bring his body into subjection the Saint fasted rigorously from his earliest years, and he never omitted this practice on a Saturday as the day specially consecrated to our Lady, whom he regarded as his Mother and particular Patroness. For devotion to her was one of his most striking characteristics, and often, when quite a little boy, his Aunt Diana used to find him out before her statue, saying the most loving things to his dear Queen.[78] But now his cousin Tobia, Diana's daughter, added fresh fuel to his ardour for God's service. She is the third woman of more than ordinary holiness whom we meet in Bernardine's life. After her husband's death, she became a tertiary of St. Francis, and managed the hospital for sick women, who were strangers at Siena. Her piety was deep and true, founded upon austerity and mortification, and Bernardine was accustomed to look upon her as his mother, seeing her very often and receiving spiritual consolation from her intercourse. Like Diana and Pia, Tobia had his innocence so much at heart that she prayed most earnestly to God to keep him free

---

[76] En Bernardinus adest.

[77] I. *Vita a Barnabaeo Senensi*, p. 726 of *Acta Sanctorum*.

[78] Ibid. p. 725.

from all evil desires and sensual love. What, therefore, was her trepidation to hear Bernardine one day say to her: 'I am in love. I should die if I could not easily see my beloved.' Sometimes he announced his intention of going to see his beloved one,' who was nobler and more beautiful than all the girls in Siena. [79] He furthermore told the troubled Tobia that he should not sleep at night if he had not looked upon the likeness of his lady during the day. She thought he was alluding to an ordinary girl, whereas he spoke of the most glorious Mother of God, whose likeness in the splendour of her Assumption he used to contemplate over one of the gates of Siena. Tobia did not guess the true object of his affections, yet seeing him persevere in his life of austere penance, she resolved to watch Bernardine,, without being seen herself, as he came in and went out of the Camelian Gate, for there, as he had once told her, he rendered homage to his lady. But her trouble was transformed into gladness when she beheld him kneeling in the joy of his heart before our Lady. Still she wished to hear the truth from Bernardine's own lips, so she said to him, 'My beloved son, I ask you not to keep me any longer in suspense, nor to let me be troubled on your account. Tell me who it is that you love, that if she be of our rank we may secure her hand for you.'

And Bernardino quickly answered: 'As you desire it, mother, I will lay open to you my secret heart as I would do to no other. I am in love with the Blessed Virgin Mary Mother of God, whom I have always cherished. Being on fire with love for her, I have espoused her as a most chaste spouse in

---

[79] Ex Analectis, p. 767.

whom I have placed all my hope. Loving and desiring her so much, I could wish to look upon her, but as I cannot obtain this grace here below, I have resolved to visit her likeness every day. So now you know who it is I love.'[80]

During the time of this holy intercourse with Tobia, Bernardine must have been living with Cristoforo and Pia till he conceived an ardent desire to join the Confraternity of Disciplinists, established at Siena, in the great hospital of Sancta Maria de Scala. It seems to have been a kind of third order, whereof the members preserved community life, and it had been the spiritual cradle of many holy men, but Bernardine became the fairest ornament of our Lady's house. There it was that uniting the consolations of prayer to the heroism of active charity he laid up a provision of strength for the terrible days of suffering which were so near. When the plague came, the brotherhood of Sancta Maria de Scala helped him to appear before the Sienese world as a 'newly rising star in the midst of a clouded time.'[81] In 1400, Siena was visited by the pestilence. It is hard in the comfortable routine of our lives to form an idea of the periodical visitations of the plague in the Middle Ages. One of its most deplorable features was the want of respect for the dead which it fostered, for so soon did the pestilence produce death and the most loathsome corruption that the nearest relatives of the deceased would allow their bodies to lie unburied till a neighbour insisted on their removal by paying a sum of money. They were then hurried into the ground without

---

[80] *Ex Analectis,* p. 767.

[81] *Ut novum sidus in opaco saeculo.*

76

any pretence of a funeral rite or ceremony. Commerce and the business of life stopped in the cities, which presented rather the appearance of churchyards, strewn with dead bodies in various stages of decay. It was a time of prosperity for those trades only which could minister to the wants of the trembling survivors, or which could help to bury speedily and with least exposure to contagion the putrid dead. In some places a tenth of the population alone survived, and we are told that Siena lost eighty thousand inhabitants in four months.[82] The Hospital of our Lady de Scala was filled with the fetid smell which this peculiar death produced. More than one hundred and forty of the brethren had succumbed in ministering to the wants of their sick, and the plague-stricken patients moaned over their lonely wretchedness. The Prior of the hospital prayed earnestly to our Lady to send him some devoted helpers, when Bernardine, who had been silently pondering over the words 'greater charity than this no man hath than to give his life for his friends,' came forward, and in the fire and freshness of his twenty years, offered himself as a willing victim to nurse the untold pains of those poor sufferers. No doubt the greatness of the sacrifice answered that secret need which he felt of giving something to God.

The Prior after he had expressed pity for the blooming youth, who in the natural order of things was going to certain death, would not oppose his desire, but established him as superintendent of the infirmary, where Bernardine's words and example

---

[82] Cantù, *Histoire des Italiens*. Traduction de M. Armand Lacombe, t. vi. p. 126.

quickly produced imitators. 'What is greater or more beautiful,' he said to his companions, 'than in time of peace to attain to the martyr's crown.' Thus by a corporal work of heroic mercy he preluded the far nobler ministry to spiritual needs which he was later to undertake. Not unfrequently it is through kindness to a sick body that access is finally obtained to the more diseased soul. The Saint spent four months at the Hospital in tender and unwearied care of its patients, applying medicaments and nursing with his own hands, and sometimes burying the dead, but although many of his companions fell victims to their charity, God did not reward him with that crown which had been perhaps an incentive to so much devotedness. When the plague had almost worked out its fury, God sent him four months of sickness exactly corresponding to the time he had spent with the sick, which unthinking men might view as a strange kind of reward for his charity, but of him it might be said that in weakness he received additional strength. When he was once more restored to health, he pondered deeply and often upon the advantages of the religious life, hesitating between the Orders of St. Dominic and St. Francis. A dream confirmed him in his own secret preference for the Friars Minor. He thought he was in a large and uncultivated field wherein stood a lofty tower. In the tower he saw a window from whence flames were issuing, and in their midst a woman with dishevelled hair and outstretched hands, who uttered thrice in a loud voice the name of Francis. The explanation of the dream seemed to point to the field as an image of the world, to the tower as God, to the flames as typifying the Holy

Spirit, whilst the woman represented the Church.[83] Bernardine resolved to become a Franciscan, but there was still another care in the world which he suffered to come between him and the accomplishment of his vocation. His father's sister, Tolla Bartolomea, was very old and infirm. Lying on her bed she would sing the divine praises with great joy, till she lost her voice, and she was so intimately united to our Lord that at the mention of the Holy Name of Jesus, she became rapt as if in ecstasy. Bernardine had always cherished her for her holiness and good counsels and now at the age of ninety-seven (another biographer makes her rather less) she was entirely helpless, not being able to move in her bed, and had become deaf and dumb. The loss of her attendant about this time was supplied by Bernardine, who waited upon her himself with patient care as long as she lived, which was more than a year. When he had closed her eyes, he retired into great solitude, where, as the prophet says, God speaks to the heart, in order to prepare for his future career. Before bidding farewell to secular life he carried out the evangelical maxim, 'If thou wilt be perfect, go sell what thou hast, and give it to the poor,'[84] lest the outward attractions of the world should bias his choice, and on the 8th of September, his twenty-second birthday, he received the habit of poverty at the hands of Father John Ristorio. This venerable Father, himself in the reputation of sanctity, had a presentiment concerning the novice's future greatness, for as he gave the poor habit and rough cord of St. Francis to Bernardine, he exclaimed,

---

83 *Vita*, p. 753.
84 St. Matt. xx. 31.

'To-day a valiant soldier is given to us who will gather most abundant fruit into the Lord's garner.'[85] Bernardine passed his year of novitiate apart from the tumult of the world in the midst of woody groves at Columbaria, a place in the neighbourhood of Siena. His brother novices seem to have been specially struck by two qualities in him, his rigorous austerity to himself, and his cordial sweetness to others, which are equally needful to an apostle. The one he fed by his constant meditation of the Passion till his heart was on fire with divine love, the second, perhaps a consequence of the first, made him eager to seek humiliating occupations for himself, and in his tenderness towards the needy, he would walk miles barefooted to carry them bread and wine. He was ordained, as it appears, shortly after his profession, though the custom of the time generally fixed the reception of the priesthood at the age of thirty. Whether it was likewise according to the practice of the age to delay the saying of Mass, we do not know, but Bernardine offered up the Holy Sacrifice for the first time a whole year after his ordination. He did not at once become famous, perhaps his intense humility kept the candlestick under the bushel. However in spite of himself, two incidents occurred which were a revelation of his mission. His loving meditation of the Passion produced in him a burning desire not only to find out what would be most pleasing to God, but also, which does not always follow, to do it whatever it might cost. In a rapture of love and ardent thirst for souls, he one day seized a heavy cross and carried it on his bare shoulders from Columbaria to Arezzo,[86]

---

85 *Vita*, p. 728.
86 *Vita*, p. 728.

and there he preached to the people in his father's tongue, that is, not so much with human science as with heavenly-inspired words after the fashion of St. Francis, his patriarch. This was a revelation, and in consequence of it he received orders to preach. But there was a natural impediment in the way of it, for Bernardine, besides his delicate health, suffered from hoarseness and could not make his voice heard. He prayed to God in simplicity to deliver him from this infirmity through the intercession of our Lady if it were really His will that he should adopt the ministry of preaching. At his prayer he seemed to see a fiery globe descend from Heaven and touch his throat, which was instantly cured.[87] And it was no dubious grace vouchsafed to him on this occasion, for afterwards we read of him that his voice was singularly sweet and clear.

Bernardine's celebrity as a preacher dates from 1418, ten years after St. Vincent's prediction and one before the death of that great servant of God. He is described as of short but upright stature. His countenance was beautiful and his appearance inspired veneration. He combined an expression of joy with one of recollection. The voice which had been given to him by a miraculous answer to prayer was full-bodied, now low, now soft and sweet, now severe and sad, and so flexible, that he had perfect control over it to direct it as and whither he would.[88] But before following Bernardine to the scene of his apostolic labours we have to ascertain the nature of the arena. If passions were powerful, what were the arms which the Saint could oppose to

---

87 *Vita*, p. 729.
88 *Vita*, p. 741.

them? Sensuality, love of money and of pleasure had perverted men's hearts from the true way. Bernardine went forth to the combat of souls from the desert of chastity and poverty, in the strength of the bare and naked Cross. As if his superiors had foreseen his future destiny, they had allotted to him the humiliating office of begging alms for the brethren from door to door. Religious superiors have a particular comprehension of the Gospel axiom, *Qui se humiliat exaltabitur.* When before Bernardine's ordination they removed him to Siena, the disagreeable nature of his employment made itself felt in proportion to the number of his old friends and acquaintances in his paternal city. Some of his relations openly disapproved of his vocation, thinking it, after the fashion of worldly minds, a dishonour to themselves, and at their secret suggestion, the little boys in the street would freely jeer at Friar Bernardine as he passed with his companion, sometimes throwing clay at his habit or stones at his bare feet. The other friar, seeing his unalterable patience, would marvel that he could allow his habit to be treated with so little respect. And Bernardine, with his sweet gentleness, would reply, 'Brother, this want of respect in those boys is not malicious but rather an effect of their youth. Leave them alone to amuse themselves that they may humble us, for much indeed would be our profit from their play if we could only gain greater patience from it. It will put us in possession of our souls and obtain for us a crown of glory.'[89]

Once when Bernardine was soliciting alms

---

[89] Chronica Seraphica del glorioso Patriarca S. Francisco de Assis, part iv. p. 469.

in his cousin Tobia's house, he was met by a relative, who burst forth into a storm of reproaches. In his words it is easy to recognize the worldly spirit which we all know so well when a vocation ceases to be a far-off theory and becomes a personal matter in a family. He marvelled how Bernardine could have the effrontery to appear before him after spoiling the hopes of his house, and choosing an idle life under the pretext of sanctity, 'for what is a friar but a pig, one who, idle himself, eats the labours of others and always looks for fat pastures.' The begging of alms 'like a hypocrite,' in other words, the humiliation of the thing, specially incensed the relative. The Saint listened to his reproaches in silence, but on this occasion he did not allow the affront offered to his habit to remain unanswered. He replied calmly that a man who embraces the Cross is no lover of idleness. 'And do not fear,' he ended by saying, 'that I shall dishonour your house, for I shall exalt it so that in all the annals of Siena no other house of rich man or potentate shall be worthier of Siena's remembrance.'[90]

Like the obedient man, the humble shall also 'speak victory,' and Bernardine spoke it on this occasion with a prophetical spirit.

---

[90] *Ex Analectis*; p. 768.

CHAPTER VII.

The Apostle of Italy.

From 1250 until the invasion of Charles VIII in 1494, the history of Italy presents an accumulation of minute facts. It was the reign of pettiness on a magnificent scale, personified now by one family or faction, now by another. Not only has it been the fate of Italy to fall a continual prey to the strongest foreign enemy— *per servir sempre, O vincitrice, O vinta* — but from the date just mentioned, Italians themselves were too prone to make the aggrandisement of their own particular territory replace a higher patriotism. The individual greatness of Italian cities and republics was superseded by the government of the tyrants, and if the licence of the first state of things had been met by democratical servitude, the resistance opposed to the tyrants was dark and underhand conspiracy. In the beginning they were chosen by the people, but with the custom of power this feature completely disappeared in their election; they preferred to buy their title of imperial vicars from the representative of the Holy Roman Empire. Thus in the fluctuating fortunes of Italy, the notion of hereditary right has been grievously wanting. Power, with certain restrictions, belonged to the strongest, to him who could best assert his claims, whilst all along the mediation of the Emperor was invoked against the preponderance of one state. The *certain restrictions* were palpable in the short-lived enjoyment of despotism which fell to the lot of many of the small princes whose elevation and deposition were alike due to a sudden revolution. In some cities, Milan, Lodi, Pavia, Brescia, and others, for instance, rival families disputed the supremacy, whilst over the whole of Italy were spread the factions of the Guelphs and Ghibellines, who fought each other, not so much in virtue of former principles as in the strength of a name which was powerful enough to keep up the fire of an ancient hatred. Ferrara, the first among Italian cities, adopted a prince in 1208, and the system of petty principalities which its example inaugurated brought about an equilibrium of power not conducive to national, but highly favourable to civil union. Upon this basis was built up the social progress of Italy for some two hundred years amid a restlessness which lived on the edge of the sword, and revelled in ignoble victories, as if without those ceaseless but quickly dispelled insurrections, life would not have been worth the living. Honest war would have been better than that perpetual dribble of skirmishes kept up by the Condottieri. They were generals who sold themselves with their companies of soldiers to the highest bidder, now fighting for, now against, the same cause, and seizing every pretext of small success to obtain higher pay. There can exist no more disturbing element to the general peace than men who live rather by the accessories of war than war itself, that is, by plundering and devastation, and the Condottieri supported through interested motives the smallest states and actions, because their own gain would rise in proportion to the number of divisions. But in Bernardine's time, besides the vigorous and grasping Republic of St. Mark, four powers in Italy were tending to a confederate unity: Lombardy, under the auspices of the Visconti, at Milan; Tuscany with Florence, its capital, and the rising Medici; the Kingdom of Naples; and the Papal States. The turbulence of the factions had driven the Pope to Avignon, and if when present he experienced so great a difficulty in holding his own, it may be gathered what his authority suffered in his absence. Albornoz, with wonderful skill, had recovered the Papal territory for his master, although he caught the Romans in the act of listening to a Roman tribune,[91] whose republican programme it was to 'judge the earth with justice and its people with equity.' Property which requires the presence and direction of an agent is a very doubtful good, and this is what the Pontifical vicars, as they were called, proved to be. Naturally the true master of the land was entirely in their power, and too often they abused their position to become practically the lord where they should have been only the lieutenant. Thus many of the towns which directly acknowledged the Holy See had become in point of fact small republics, about whose municipal privileges the inhabitants were exceedingly jealous. It was this strong individuality in the Italian character which retarded Italy's political unity, yet without the party spirit and the factions it would have been a very prosperous time as to comfort, wealth, and independence. For the Italians we might change one word of St. Augustine's definition of strength.[92] For them it would have been order in liberty. The sins of those days against which all St. Bernardine's efforts as an apostle were directed, are those of an overgrown civilization, produced though it was in this case by individual efforts. Italy, says one of the foremost of her historians,[93] was about to pass from the ages of faith to a political era. We can

---

[91] Cola di Rienzo.

[92] Virtus est ordo amoris.

[93] Cesare Cantù.

understand that the exaggeration of an unpractising faith will often result in gross superstition, and that this superstition will sometimes mar the face of truth with its own unwise conceits. Perhaps this is exemplified in the way the plague, which hangs like a dark curtain over the closing scene of the Middle Ages, was viewed by various minds. Some saw in it a punishment for the violation of Sunday and feast-days, a curse upon blasphemy, usury, and adultery; and the exaggeration of faith broke forth in a somewhat cut and dried routine of processions, exorcisms, and pretended miracles, whilst on the other hand, panic produced a craving to eat, drink, and be merry, which was wild in its intensity. The Dances of the Dead set forth in popular paintings the weird spectacle of death and enjoyment. The whole scene of popes, kings, merchants, writers, old men and young, women and children, who join hands in the dance, though some of them are only skeletons, seem to say, 'Let us cover ourselves with roses.[94] Poor plague-stricken people! Whether they would or not, death was at hand, and whilst they acknowledged the warning of the plague, their hearts were far from the faith of their lips. It is in vain to oppose sin with the letter of religion.

Now Bernardine's apostolate vigorously attacked the habit of usury, gambling, and the refinement of luxury in women's dress, three things which come under the same head and are noticeable in an effete society, also the bitter enmity produced by the factions, and immorality. There was something solid about the trophies which he carried away from the battlefield. They were those

---

94

funeral piles of feminine adornments which he laid upon the altar of sacrifice, those unmistakeable symptoms of a returning brotherly love, or those galling public penances which were generously undertaken at his voice in virtue of that Holy Name he loved so tenderly.

In 1378 Siena, which was renowned for its democratical traditions and governed at that time by its Council of Nine, had renounced its natural and Guelph ally, Florence, to sign a league with Giovanni Galeazzo Visconti, the then rising star of Italian skies, and it was at Milan, the capital of the Visconti, in 1418 or 1420, for there is some uncertainty as to date, that Bernardine began to be famous, although he had then been preaching for the space of fourteen years in various parts. He emulated St. Vincent in his mode of life, going from place to place with a chaste yet fiery eloquence, which fell like burning coals upon the chilled hearts of the Italian people. Before it was light his congregation gathered together in the place appointed for the sermon, and even quite little children were taken by their parents, as if the mere sight of the Saint would bring down a blessing upon their future life. Every day, after devoutly celebrating the Holy Sacrifice, he preached to the crowds who gathered from the neighbouring towns and villages to hear him. 'The world,' says Bernardine's biographer, that is, his Italian world probably, 'seethed with magical arts and sacrileges. Incantations were used to cure illness, and the men of that age, reading future events by divination, and dealing in the prognostics of magic, deceived their fellow men. Mass on festival-days was rarely heard, the Sacrament of Penance, with the Sacred Body of

Christ, received only once a year, or oftener men contented themselves with a death-bed confession and Communion. There was no fear of laws which prohibited games of chance; the dice- players boldly assembled in public gymnasiums, where they could give themselves up to their play with impunity. No distinction was apparent between festival and other days, excepting, perhaps, in the greater concourse of people to witness the various performances.'[95] The Saint appeared in the midst of this complete forgetfulness of God, and urged upon each one the duty of individual efforts of penance, that so the Divine anger might be appeased. Many persons returned indeed to the practices of the faith, or adopted them, who had either given up going to the sacraments or never made an effort in that direction. *Et emitte coelitus lucis tuae radium*, the Church sings in her beautiful sequence to the Holy Spirit. Certain saints seem to set forth in their working the answer to this petition. A devout woman at Arezzo often saw a globe of various colours issuing as if with the breath from Bernardine's mouth when he was preaching, and once a good but lukewarm youth came to consult him as to whether he should enter religion. 'You must pray to God about this, my son,' answered the Saint, ' that He may inspire you for the greater good of your soul.' Whilst saying this he laid his hand upon the youth's arm, and although the weather was exceedingly cold, the touch seemed like fire. What does this signify, adds the biographer, but that cold hearts were fired by his speech and by his touch.[96] His character appears in all its ripe beauty

---

[95] *Vita*, p. 729.

[96] *Vita*, p. 731.

as we find him at Milan preaching with evangelical courage before a tyrant, then its Duke, Filippo Maria Visconti. It seems that the Saint had been moved by inspiration to visit Lombardy, and when he arrived at Milan, he found its people too obsequious in their flattery of the Duke, speaking to him on bended knee as if he had been a god. Bernardine attacked this vanity in one of his sermons, and although he did it in a general way, the Duke took offence, and declared that no more such sermons should be preached, or the preacher should suffer. Bernardine answered that it was his duty to combat vices, not to offend individuals, that far from laying down his arms so easily, he should esteem himself happy to bear witness to the truth. The Duke said no more then, but his spirit was angered, and when one of his servants came to him as a tempter, proposing to lay a bait for the friar's virtue, he readily yielded to the counsel. The servant, like most of his kind, evidently knew human nature. 'Perhaps this friar,' he tentatively said to the Duke, 'who is so austere, and preaches so strongly in disfavour of riches, would appreciate them better if he saw and felt them than he does now that they are at a distance. Try him with money: his acceptance or rejection of it will give us his measure.' The Duke made use of this cunning servant to send Friar Bernardine five hundred florins, with the request that he would spend them on himself. Living at the cost of Divine Providence, the Saint said that he wanted nothing, but Milan possessed many poor, who would be only too glad of the alms. This answer did not suit the malicious servant, and he returned once more to Bernardine, begging him to accept the Duke's bounty. 'I must not return to my Lord with the florins, Father,' he alleged, 'and you will vex him if you do not take his gift.' The Saint was fully conscious of the tempter. Turning to him, he replied, 'If that is the case, I wish to employ his money as best I can. Follow me.' They went out to the prison, where Bernardine speedily ascertained those who were detained for debt, and charged the servant to see how far the money would go. Two prisoners alone, whom it did not suffice to rescue, wept bitterly at the Saint's feet. He said tenderly, 'My children, I have no more to give you, but I will stake my influence to procure your liberty, and if I cannot obtain sufficient money, I offer myself as a prisoner that you may be freed.' 'Now tell the Duke,' he added to the servant, 'that in his name, and merely to please him, I took his money; and tell him how I spent it, and that I appeal to his generosity to deliver me from the obligation of my promise to rescue those two poor prisoners. My personal liberty depends upon their debts, because I am so honourable a man that if they are not freed, I shall keep my word.' The servant returned in confusion to his master, whereas the Duke exclaimed, 'I wish to be the friend of so chivalrous a man,' and willingly paid the debt.[97] This sweetness exhibited towards a temporal suffering was a figure of the far greater anxiety felt by the Saint to rescue sinners under the thraldom of vice. Solicitude for a soul's spiritual imprisonment will often prove to be the first chord which strikes home to the hardened heart after the erring of many years, and produces at last from it that cry of the Psalmist, 'The net is broken and we are free.' Bernardine found Milan steeped in vice, but an old chronicle says that he planted the standard of virtue with so vigorous a hand that even

---

[97] *Chronica*, p. 481.

in the captain's absence the soldiers he had trained remained true to their colours.[98]

His apostolate spread itself over a period of thirty-eight years, of which the first ten or fourteen were passed in obscurity. Bernardine was the Apostle of Italy, and all his labours without exception belonged to Italy. In the year 1420 he was at Piacenza, Bergamo, and Brescia; in 1422 at Verona and Venice on a mission of peace; in 1423 at Vicenza, 1427 in Rome, 1429 at Liguria, Genoa, Savona, Milan; in 1432, at Siena and Rome; in 1433 at Siena, occupied in arranging his works; in 1438 he was elected Vicar of the Convents of the Primitive Observance,[99] and was at Naples and Aquila; in 1440 at Florence, 1443 at Ferrara, where he predicted the misfortunes which were to fall upon Italy in 1510 and 1511. In 1444 he was in the Kingdom of Naples, at Massa, the city of his birth, and at Siena for the last time. He was wending his way from Spoleto to Aquila when a mortal sickness overtook him at his post and in his armour.[100] He inaugurated a new method of preaching, for the decay which had affected other practices of religion was visible too in the pulpit. It is said that, if in denouncing vice he excelled all contemporary preachers, in speaking of our Lady he surpassed

---

[98] *Chronica*, p. 481.

[99] The Franciscan Order was divided into two principal branches at the time of the Council of Constance: the Observants, and the Conventuals. Other reforms were — (1) the Minorites of the Observance of Paoletto da Foligno, 1368; (2) the Brothers of the Strict Observance of John de la Puebla, 1469; (3) the Discalced Capuchins, 1496 (Hergenröther, *Kirchengeschichte* II. B. p.149).

[100] In Commentario, p. 723.

himself.[101]

There is something most touchingly poetical about Bernardine's first encounter after leaving Milan. He was travelling on foot with one companion when dark night overtook them in the solitude of a mountain pass, and they lost their way. The Saint's companion was appalled by the loneliness of the place and its solitude, but Bernardine stayed his fears by the thought of that Divine Providence Whose arms were round them. The barking of a dog, which they soon heard, apprised them of rescue, and they walked on till they came to a small dwelling belonging to a labourer, who received them, notwithstanding the inopportune hour, with much hospitality. But when he discovered that one of his guests was Friar Bernardine, he called all the members of his family, that each one might benefit by the visit of a holy man, and left nothing undone which could refresh the weary travellers. The Saint was never outdone in generosity. He thanked the labourer by an earnest prayer to God to bless him with plenty and prosperity, and the request was granted, for later on the popular voice attributed these temporal blessings to the Saint's visit in the phrase, 'the family blessed by St. Bernardine.'[102]

On his way to Mantua, where he was to preach in the following year, 1419, he had to traverse a river at high tide, and possessed not wherewith to pay the ferryman. The man, seeing the poverty apparent in the Saint's habit and that of

---

[101] *Vita*, p. 731.
[102] "La familia bendita de San Bernardino" (*Chronica*, p. 483).

his companion, insisted upon his money there and then, saying that the prayer, which Bernardine promised him in return for a free passage, would not enable him to live. Then the Saint besought him with humility to count upon a collection which he was going to make at Mantua. 'Father,' answered the man, 'the people there can go without their sermon much better than I without my money,' and he still refused. Then Bernardine turned to his companion, saying, 'Brother, have you confidence in God, and have you sufficient courage and faith to do as you shall see me do? '

'Yes, Father.'

'Then in virtue of the most sweet Name of Jesus, Whom the elements obey, follow me.' Stretching his cloak over the waters, they walked across the river as if they had been on dry land, followed shortly by the contrite ferryman in his boat. He begged the Saint's forgiveness, and when Bernardine asked him to keep the miracle a secret, he replied frankly, 'No, Father, it would be ingratitude to God if I did not atone for my sin by some public confession and penance, that men may know I am so bad that I obliged God, as it were, to work this great miracle.'[103]

The fame of what he had done helped on Bernardine's mission at Mantua, as it may be supposed. In the course of the same journey the Apostle came upon a dead man who lay bathed in his blood, the victim, perhaps, of the party spirit which was often helped to execute its wicked deeds

---

[103] *Chronica*, p. 484.

by those mountain passes. Bernardine called him back to life by the invocation of the Name of Jesus, that power which he evoked so opportunely over the feuds of the times.

There is something very significant in the special devotion of a great saint. In this case it answered the spiritual needs of those days in Italy, for if men were so prone to strife and cruelty because of the name of Guelph or Ghibelline, which no longer signified anything beyond the particular interest of the individual, the name of Jesus is the emblem of peace, charity, and holiness. For Bernardine it was later to be the sign set up by God to work him contradiction. 'O thou Name of Jesus,' he breaks forth in one of his sermons, 'exalted above every name! O triumphant Name! O joy of angels and of the just! O fear of Hell! In Thee is all hope of pardon, of grace, and of glory. O most sweet Name! Thou givest pardon to sinners, Thou dost renovate us, Thou dost fill our hearts with divine sweetness, and dost expel our fears. O Name full of grace! through Thee the perception of great mysteries is attained, and souls are inflamed with divine love, are strengthened in their combats, and delivered from all evils.'[104] In many of the places visited by the Saint, party spirit had set up its badges at the tops of houses, gates, and public places, and sometimes introduced them into churches, for factions formed a kind of freemasonry, whereof the members were gradually substituting the promptings of wild passion, with its outward signs, for the *Credo*, and for the rites and ceremonies of the true faith. Bernardine, then, caused the Holy Name to be

---

[104] Sermo III. In Epiphania Domini.

engraved on a wooden tablet in letters of gold, and he was in the habit of holding this symbol up to the people after his sermon. Three towns in particular seem to have been most cruelly divided by the spirit of hatred — Verona, Perugia, and Bergamo. At Verona, where the Saint preached in 1422, he found the Guelphs and Ghibellines in open war, and the streets streaming with the blood of the combatants. Bernardine's mission was crowned by a general making of peace, and a procession of thanksgiving, which procession the grateful inhabitants renewed for many years afterwards.[105] On one occasion at Perugia the people, armed with iron helmets, and conspicuous with badges of owl or oxen, according to their party, fought each other with a misplaced zeal, many losing their lives in the unworthy struggle, and becoming the 'devil's martyrs.' [106] Bernardine quickly stopped these warlike proceedings, and at his words the signs of owls and of oxen, together with the extraordinary articles of feminine apparel, which never escaped his vigilance, were brought to the pile and consumed. 'The Lord God,' he said at another time to the same people, 'considering that fatal spirit which He hates above everything, has sent me to you as His angel to announce peace on earth unto those men amongst you who are of good will. You who desire peace, proposing to keep it henceforth with your neighbour, come to my right hand, and you who desire it not, stand on my left.' All save one young nobleman with his followers moved to the Saint's right, but he, murmuring against Bernardine, kept to the left side. Knowing the

---

[105] *Chronica*, p. 484.

[106] *Ex Analectis*, p. 771.

weight of evil example, the apostle admonished him publicly to forgiveness of the injuries he had received, 'for if thou dost not promise to keep the peace thou shalt not enter thy house alive.' But the nobleman reviled the prophetic words, and as he was crossing the threshold of his door fell suddenly dead.[107]

Sometimes Bernardine chose a humorous mode of dealing with the spirit of contention. Thus he once excited the people's curiosity for many days by the announcement that he would show them the devil. When therefore a multitude had gathered itself together in expectant awe, he said, 'Now I will keep my word, and whereas I promised to show you one devil I will show you many. Look you one at another, and thus you will see devils, for you yourselves are devils, doing his work."[108]

Is there not a great merit in this plain speaking, and how, we ask, without the salutary doctrine of eternal punishment, is the fear of God ever to be produced in the hearts of wicked and depraved men? The great majority are moved by threats rather than by love, so that we may fear many reach only attrition and stop short of contrition, to their own great loss. The state of mind which does not tolerate the doctrine of eternal punishment is near akin to that which denies the basis of all religion, the doctrine of God the Creator.

Perhaps it was at one of these towns that Bernardine preached his three famous sermons

---

[107] *Analecta*, p. 771.
[108] Ibid.

against the spirit of faction. It finds less echo in our own times than another abuse against which he was loud in his denunciation, but the race of men who seek nothing but their own interests under the shadow of a great name is by no means extinct. Bernardine denounces them with remarkable sagacity, seeing that their party spirit was an infusion of the old idolatry into Christian society. In reading what he preached in the full light of his own Catholic faith to Italians of the fifteenth century, we may draw our conclusions as to how he would stigmatize the modern deification of human reason, with its accompaniments of a world-soul in the place of God, with its abolition of hell-fire and the legions of devils, treating the one as an invention of man and the other as a hideous fable. A man in the emancipation of the nineteenth century surely bears about him something like those badges of owls and oxen; created as a reasonable being, he walks upon the earth purblind as an owl, or dull as an ox.

It was Bernardine's custom to preach at great length, and to divide his sermons into articles, which he again subdivided into points. As we read we are convinced of the patriotic heart which must have dictated those ardent words about the troubles of Italy. One of these sermons is for the third Sunday in Lent, and is on the text, 'Every kingdom divided against itself shall fall.' It bears the heading, 'against the Guelphs and Ghibellines and other productions of party spirit,' 'Where is the man of heart so hard and so stony, that he could refrain from tears if he were to have knowledge of the things which we have heard, and seen, and known by certain experience, in the regions of Italy, and above all in Lombardy?' [109] Then he proves his words, showing how factions lead to the destruction of the country. 'When parties begin to boil over, their sins require punishment: the devil brings it about, and Divine justice permits that one banishes the other. The goods of the exiles are pillaged, 'their homes destroyed, their lands go uncultivated, their vineyards are cut down and destroyed, the arts and commerce are given up by them, their herds and flocks and other live stock are devoured. The lads sent into banishment with their fathers are obliged by want to let themselves out for hire. They become thieves; some are hung, some are killed, some perish in battle, others end a miserable life by some other kind of unhappy death. The young men do not marry, and live in the same way as those just mentioned. The marriageable girls remain without husbands; some take to a wandering life and to the worst of trades. The men are worn out by hunger, poverty, sadness, and manifold misery, and they wander wretchedly from place to place. Religious lose their regular observance, clerics lay aside the modesty of their state, learning and study are abandoned. Cities become dens of thieves, churches are profaned, monasteries de-peopled and ruined, wives are made widows, and all goods temporal and spiritual are destroyed. But this is not the end of evils. There remain "other five." When the sins of the banished party have been punished, and the wickednesses of the party which expelled it have reached their full height, then there is another crash of Divine justice, and the wheel of the state of worldly affairs turns round. The banished come

---

[109] *Dominica III. in Quad.* In exordio.

back, and drive out those who were in power; they revenge themselves with savage cruelty, and pay off the score of all the injuries which they have received. *If anything remains to be destroyed, the end of its destruction is at hand.*' What wonder indeed that the Pope should have appreciated the peace of Avignon. 'I have seen,' adds the Saint, in finishing this point, 'two cocks fighting a long and severe battle together, tearing one another to pieces with beaks and spurs, and when they were both utterly exhausted, and could fight no more, their rage against one another had not diminished but increased. And so I have seen many of these faction men, so utterly wretched as to have wasted their whole substance upon their feuds, and to have nothing at all left except the rabid fury of their party spirit.' These men, according to Bernardine's recommendation, were to be avoided like the pestilence. Of both corporal and spiritual plague he could say, *experto credite*. He finishes the point by these strong words, 'Perhaps some are surprised that I speak so severely against these parties, but the answer is supplied by sad experience. The plague comes into a city and many die, but many remain alive, and generally they are the larger part. But let the faction of Guelphs or Ghibellines, or any other, enter a city, and it is the greatest wonder if any escape, without at least in course of time joining, or being thought to join, one side or the other, as I indeed, to my astonishment and surprise, know from certain experience. And, what is most of all to be grieved over, even those who seem to fear God become so mad and senseless, especially where the Guelphs and Ghibellines are concerned, that they live as serenely in their faction as if the perfection of sanctity consisted in it. They are like Lot's sons-in-law in Sodom, who were so utterly without sense of the wickedness of the place, that when he endeavoured to persuade them to depart he seemed to them to be jesting.'[110] Bernardine here gives one of the reasons for that moral decline in Italy which came more particularly under his notice as an apostle. In the sermon which follows for the same day he goes into more particulars, it being directed against the signs or badges of the parties, and he quotes the text of the thirty-seventh Psalm, 'They have set up their ensigns for badges.' He denounces these badges as marks of idolatry, and the using them as a sin which kills the soul, and he gives a noticeable reason why Italy amongst all other nations should suffer from this party spirit. 'When the Apostles and Disciples preached the Most Holy Name of Jesus Christ, demons fled from the idols, images were reduced to dust, and all pestilent idolatry was destroyed in virtue of the martyrdom of the Saints. The same envy which brought death into the world, the faith of Christians being cold, has set up idolatry again in Italy, though in a more hidden way. For, as if in derision of Christ and of His Church, in that spot where the Roman Empire, the principal seat of idolatry, had reigned, and later, at the prayer of Christ, the indefectible Chair of Peter, in that very place idolatry has been renewed by the agency of the devil, for this is done by using party badges. The Apostle foresaw this when he wrote to the Romans who are in Italy, Rome being the capital of Italy and the Chair of Peter. In the first chapter to the Romans he thus speaks of the idolatry which we now see, 'Because that when they

---

[110] De impiis partialitatibus (Sermo xxv. p. 110 and following).

knew God, they have not glorified Him as God, or given thanks, but became vain in their thoughts, and their foolish heart was darkened. For professing themselves to be wise they became fools. And they changed the glory of the incorruptible God into the likeness of the image of a corruptible man, and of birds and of four-footed beasts and of creeping things.'[111] Now our own experience tells us that this is literally true. Some of these parties have as the standard of their faction a man who is their head, whom they follow and honour more than God, for whom they willingly die, which they will not do for Christ; and this man is the image, not of God, but of a corruptible man, a very devil incarnate. Some have birds for badges, such as eagles of various colours, or other live birds, which they feed like idols. Others have four-footed animals. Some have a lion of ordinary colour, some a white one, a red one, and so on. Some honour serpents. I would not condemn arms or badges of nobles or republics, in so far as they are not party signs, because men may wear them without sinning if they bear them without passion. But for the greater part their use is abused, and they become party badges. For instance, the eagle, as denoting the imperial dignity, is by no means Ghibelline, but is adopted in Italy by the Ghibellines. Some insane men, moreover, assert that the Church is Guelph, but, as experience teaches us, the Guelphs will fight for their own interest seven times a day against the Church, and the Ghibellines for their own interest seven times a day against the Empire. For, as the Apostle says, 'all such men seek their own interests, not those of Jesus Christ.' In their absurdity, the Saint goes on to

---

[111] Romans i. 21 — 23.

remark, they make a certain saint a Guelph and another a Ghibelline, and worse than this they make the very God of eternal peace belong to one of their parties. 'But alas! alas! and again alas!' bursts from Bernardine's lips as he speaks of the devotedness of these men to their faction, who will not bear a blow on their cheek for the love of our Lord; who will punish with relentless vengeance and with death the smallest insult offered to their badge, and will not raise their finger to punish contempt towards God, our Lady, and the Saints. In Lombardy they have surpassed the old persecutors of the martyrs, by devouring the cooked flesh =of their victims. Well might Bernardine sigh, 'Alas! alas! and again alas!' over the evils opposed to the virtue essentially Christian by the factions, over that imitation of idolatry, that adoration of the devil, and that truly demoniacal vengeance.[112] At another time he divides his sermon against the same evil into three parts, suggested by the text, 'Woe, woe, woe unto the inhabitants of the earth.' The first *woe* is directed against those who belong to a faction in their hearts, the second against those whose actions favour this wretched and soul-destroying spirit. He overthrows the objections of those who allege that their ancestors belonged to this or that party, or that certain states and cities impose an oath of obedience to one particular faction, and he gives a most horrible picture of a country exposed to these divisions. 'If any man be in doubt regarding this, let him attentively consider the consequences of party strife. They are prohibitions, betrayals, murder, fire, tyranny, the seeds of discord, the oppression of innocence, impious calumnies, hatred, revenge,

---

[112] *Contra partialitatum insignia* (Sermo xxvi. v. i. p. 115).

false accusations, injustice, employment given to unworthy subjects, the division of friends, relations, comrades, parents, and children.'[113] This is, as it were, the bare outline of the evils which the Saint further develops, but his words already quoted are sufficient to prove how much Italy needed an apostle.

The second great evil which called for this energetic voice was gambling, or the passion for games of chance, and very probably this was one of the causes of the very prevalent usury of the day. It can easily be understood that the one engenders the other, as an unlawful mode of spending money will suggest all kinds of ways of making it. Bernardine compares gambling to a kind of rival Catholic Church of the powers of darkness. He supposes the devil to be calling together his satellites at the sound of the trumpet, and he puts these words into his mouth: 'I have learnt by your account that Christ our Adversary has established one Holy Church on earth for the salvation of souls. Now I have been thinking of establishing a rival Church for the wicked in order to lose souls, and whatever He instituted in His Church unto good, I will disorganize it in mine unto evil. The gambling-houses, to be set up as near as possible to the true temples of God, are to be the rival attraction to the services of the Church, and they are to promote sensuality by providing savoury food, greediness being so often the first incentive to a life of vice.' The devil's wish, for in the first point the Saint speaks quaintly enough in his words, is to succeed in getting a greater attendance in his 'profane

---

[113] *De partialitatibus* (Sermo xxv. vol. ii. p. 143).

churches' than our Lord gains in His. The gambling tables represent ecclesiastical fittings and ornaments, and the dice stand for the missal. Obscene pictures form this breviary of impiety, and open the minds of the gamblers to knowledge of the most horrible vice. 'The more wicked they are, the dearer they will be to me.' The third comparison of the ceremonies of the Mass to those of the gambling-tables, though somewhat fanciful, gives us an insight to the sort of impiety which was carried on under the cloak of a passion apparently distinct from it. Fifteen grievous sins, according to St. Bernardine, arise from indulgence in gambling, and one of the not least deadly of its results is idleness, and idleness was one of the crimes which ruined Sodom. 'Gamblers become sensual, degenerate, and reprobate, and their life sets the first counsel of the law at defiance, to live honestly. I heard from one who was worthy of credence, that having once lost all he had at gambling, he played for and lost his teeth, and suffered them to be pulled out with equanimity. Another man pledged and lost his wife twice, and would have made her over to the winner had not some good woman befriended her for the love of God.'[114]

In connection with this propensity to gambling a very pleasing anecdote is told of Bernardine's sojourn at Bologna, where the passion for card playing was most rife. The Saint had probably preached with his usual unction, for he had persuaded the ringleaders to bring their cards to the altar of sacrifice. But one young man, who supported his wife and a large family by painting

---

[114] *De alcarum ludo* (Sermo xlii. v. i. p. 195).

cards, found himself thus deprived of the means of sustenance, and came to expose his distress to Bernardine. 'Be not anxious,' answered the Saint, 'for I will give you a more fitting subject for your pencil, and one which will be more lucrative too.' Taking a pen, he drew with it the favourite subject of his thoughts, a sun bearing in its centre the Holy Name of Jesus, promising the man that he should not lose by this new trade. The event proved the truth of his words, for so great was the devotion enkindled by his preaching, that every one wished to possess a tablet with the life-giving name, and the former card-painter became a very prosperous man.[115] It must be owned that St. Paul's assertion, 'Godliness is profitable to all things' seldom receives so clear an illustration.

And now to come to luxury in dress, which failing has more to say to our own times than the Guelphs and Ghibellines, or even the gambling tables. Bernardine dealt powerfully with the exaggerated taste of the day for finery, using unmistakeably strong language to speak his own thoughts on the subject. He saw indeed in the habit of mind which displayed so great a solicitude about its body's garments an utter disregard of souls, or a deliberate wish to entrap them, and this it was that aroused all the fire of his apostolic spirit. What he says is in many respects so pertinent, that the inclination to quote largely from his sermons is only too tempting. 'The evils resulting from vanity,' he says, 'affect four classes of persons — parents, married people, artisans, the accomplices of vanity,' and he attacks most vigorously that particular kind

---

[115] *Chronica*, p. 485.

of worldliness in parents which seeks after brilliant marriages for their daughters, regardless of cost or means, provided the end is attained. We leave our readers to judge whether this quality is obsolete. 'How many crimes do you not commit, O unhappy mother, that your daughter may please all who look upon her? How anxiously do you strive to add other advantages to those which nature has bestowed upon her! If she is too lean, you try to make her appear fatter; and if she is too fat, you squeeze her; if she is born crooked, you contract her to make her straight. You teach her to dress her head, to paint her face, to walk elegantly, to find out new fashions, and to sing love-songs. What more can I say? You yourself are an experienced mistress of worldly arts to your daughter, and you care not at all for the good of her soul. Oh, what madness! But you, fathers of daughters, now I speak to you. You enrich yourselves only too well by means of theft, usury, and in other abominable ways, that you may marry your daughters magnificently, and gain them a high position. But what is worse in parents is this: when they marry their daughter, they do not consider whether they are giving her to an honest man, but they think only of one thing, whether they are giving her to a rich man that she may shine. O unwise parents, hastening to eternal damnation for your daughters' sake, and taking them with you! O worldly-wise parents, destroyers of your own souls and of your children's!' Further on in the same sermon he speaks of worse evils arising from this fatal desire to shine in the world. First of all, those who might marry are afraid of taking wives with tastes so expensive, and they remain unmarried to lead immoral and vicious lives. Then very often parents exhaust all their resources upon one or two

107

daughters who are pretty, and the others remain at home, though not indeed to preserve their innocence; or worse still, if they happen to have any deformity, they are sent into a convent, 'like the scum or the refuse of the world.'[116] In this way the beauty of a religious vocation is disfigured, and little by little the holiest of things is turned into derision. The dregs of the chalice are thrown to God. In sorrow of heart the Apostle of Italy alludes to this system, destructive to national and social prosperity, 'I would rather keep silence than speak of these things,' but still, with a trembling hand, he lifts up the veil which outward decorum, at least, holds over life-destroying vice.[117]

In another sermon Bernardine goes into somewhat amusing details in the various departments of feminine vanity. First, as to paint and false hair, the wearing of which he denounces as mortal sin. Secondly, he has a particular aversion to dresses with long tails, for in his day, as it appears from his sermons, much waste was occasioned in this way, owing to the very costly materials of the said tails. Thirdly, the erections worn by women on their heads, and these he likens to a crown, not of twelve stars, but of twelve foolishnesses. His description of the tail is quaint, and also interesting, as a costume portrait of the period: 'Our experience tells us that these tails are nothing else but the multiplication of evil expenses, the similitude of an animal, muddy in winter, dusty in summer, a broom of fools, an infernal censer, a peacock in the mud, a cause of blasphemy, the rapacity of pride, a serpent

---

[116] Quasi spumam vel vomitum saeculi.
[117] *De malis ex vanitate* (Sermo xlvi. v. i. p. 213).

of hell, a chariot of devils, and a blood-stained sword of Satan's.' But the abuses of this item are no fewer than twelve, which Bernardine enumerates: 'The first abuse is the multiplication of unnecessary expenses. Think, O unhappy woman with a tail, how much expense is incurred by your trains.' The length and expensive quality of the material are alluded to, and besides sweeping up the dust and mud, the tail, according to Bernardine, is often purchased with the blood of the poor, and hence draws down a curse upon its wearers. Whereas a beast has but one tail, a woman sometimes chooses to have seven or more, and she had better follow out the similitude and go on all fours. Then what impatience the same tail causes her maid, who has to brush it when it is taken off after having paraded the dusty streets. What a source of temptation it is to the poor to behold mud, as it were, clothed in fine garments, whilst they are tormented by cold, hunger, and thirst. 'You will rarely find one of these luxurious women,' says Bernardine, 'with a heart open to the needs of the poor.' But a worse abuse, as it seems to us, is that painful striving of every class to exalt itself out of its own sphere by adopting an unsuitable style of dress. The Saint uses the comparison of the different members of the heavenly hierarchy to exemplify the absurdity of these pretensions. 'Why in the lowest of women is there a perfect passion to emulate the trains of empresses, queens, and duchesses? What is this but inordinate pride? What if the nose should usurp the place of the ear or the eye in the human face, would it not be monstrous?' When he reaches the third point, the false hair and the head-dresses, he breaks forth into a comparison between the Christian woman who thus decks herself out, and the. Divine

Head of our Lord, crowned with thorns. 'It would seem strange indeed if a woman who had just lost her husband or father went to Mass with her head adorned with flowers. But it is much more strange if a woman redeemed by Christ's Blood, the daughter and spouse of the Eternal Father, go to Mass not only with flowers in her hair, but with gold, precious stones, paint, and false hair. For every Mass is celebrated unto a remembrance of the suffering Christ, and when the priest elevates the Body and Blood of Christ, the elevation of His Body on the Cross is commemorated. O vanity of woman, which decks out the head with so great a variety of ornaments! Be mindful of that Divine Head, revered by the angels, which is pierced to its marrow by thorns, and covered with Blood for the expiation of your vanity; but yours is graced by every possible adornment. That Head is crowned with thorns, yours with precious stones. His Hair- is bloody; yours — or I should say, another's — is whitened by artifice. His Face is disfigured by pallor, spittle, and blood; yours with paint of various hues. Those beautiful Eyes, which the angels contemplate, are obscured by a most bitter death ; yours are on fire with luxury and concupiscence.'[118]

Elsewhere he ridicules women who will wear the hair of a dead person, because the devil prevents them from thinking about it, whereas they would be terrified to carry on their heads one single bone of a dead man.[119]

---

[118] *Contra fucatas* (Sermo xlvii. v. i. p. 217).

[119] *De Maria Magdalena, et de bonis et malis mulieribus* (Sermo xxxviii. v. iii. p. 268).

We would call attention to one more point on this chapter of women's dress. It is the whole system of deceit, that is, of resorting to artificial means to supply natural deficiencies, which the Saint denounces in the same satirical but straightforward terms. Women come under this category who 'paint their faces, and wish to make themselves either taller or better-looking than they really are, who pad themselves out to appear good figures, . . . such women always commit mortal sin.' And there follows a recommendation to unmarried women to be candid with their future husbands, if they have any natural defects. 'If you are lame, you can hide your lameness after you are married, but you are bound to make known your natural shortcomings before marriage, lest your husband be deceived in his merchandise. And do not imitate a certain little woman who, wishing to marry, ordered herself an enormous pair of high shoes, and an immense erection of back hair, and padded herself with silk, so that she might appear to be plump and well-formed, although in reality she was somewhat hump-backed. After her marriage, when the high-heeled shoes and back hair were taken off, she looked so small, that her husband thought she was kneeling, and said, "Get up off your knees," but when he found out what she was, he would have nothing more to do with her. Lastly, a vain woman deceives her confessor, for when he asks her, "Wherefore all this vanity in your person?" she answers, "To please my husband," and she lies, because he sees her at home, not only without her adornments, but sometimes untidy and uncombed, and whereas she goes forth to make herself pleasant to others, he cannot succeed in getting even a good word out of her.'[120]

The words of St. Bernardine open a curious vista upon the weaknesses and vices of his day, but frivolous as the women must have been to whom he addressed this satirical yet humorous preaching, we venture to say that in one respect at least they were better Christians than we are in these days of compromises. In many cases we read that the articles of finery, to which the Saint makes so many unmerciful allusions, were brought to the fire and burnt. Attempts to serve God and Mammon were less frequent than now, and if vice was rife, penance was not shirked. We do not know that St. Bernardine had ever occasion to say, as Father Faber says, 'If you dance till four in the morning, and go to Communion at ten, I do not believe in your abiding sorrow for sin. If you are in the theatre till midnight, I do not credit the compunction of your morning's meditation.' [121] In spite of an overwhelming luxury in dress, the spirit of the middle ages had not died out, it produced one grand result: men were rather ashamed of their sin than of its penance.

---

[120] *De domino, honesta* (Sermo xxxv. v. ii. p. 259).
[121] *Spiritual Conferences*, p. 356.

CHAPTER VIII.

To suffer ignominy for the Name of Jesus.

The Saint who possessed so much practical knowledge of the evils which he fought against, probably owed some of his inspirations to Capriola, a monastery of the Observance in the neighbourhood of Siena, whither he retired from time to time to merge the preacher in the friar. Obedience and silent communings with God were his rest, the oasis of his ministry, for there is an absence of hurry, a calmness about the occupations of the busiest saints which is not one of the least marks of holiness. They made unto themselves inner lives independent of outward circumstances, so that when God saw well to alter these, or even to take away what might seem to be the daily bread of their working faculties, they proved happiness to be distinct from all this, and realized the observation of a great thinker,[122] who says that it is in us and in God. To solitude, represented in Bernardine's life by the quiet of Capriola, may perhaps be attributed his peaceful confidence in the midst of persecution.

'More deserving of admiration than of imitation' is a phrase often used in speaking of some heroic action in a saint, and its purport is fully exemplified when a man undertakes what a saint undertook before him, but without the special call from God to do it. We have seen how faithfully the bands who followed St. Vincent Ferrer from place to place both answered his invitation to penance and inspired contrition in others. If this system of

---

[122] Pascal. *Pensées.*

conversion had been an abnormal remedy, there was no want of natural wisdom about the whole plan, and the law of God was strictly carried out before pilgrims were allowed to think of a work of supererogation. The case entirely changes when an ordinary man, without special call, adopts an extraordinary course of life. He falls into the natural snares which the Saint avoided, because he was doing an appointed work, and there is a want of common sense on the face of the whole matter which it is humiliating to realize. In the days of St. Gregory the Great men then living fancied they should see the end; at the extreme confines of the middle ages the same idea was prevalent, or rather fear of the end was fear of the personal Antichrist, and if a saint such as St. Vincent Ferrer had wrought a plentiful harvest for God as the Apostle of the Judgment, others without his sanctity traded deceitfully with the popular belief, and made up to themselves not treasures in Heaven but infatuated followers on earth. God allowed one of these to perfect His servant Bernardine in suffering ignominy for His name's sake. A certain Manfred de Vercelli, a Dominican as it seems, a friar of great learning, but of too much credulity, was actively preaching the speedy coming of Antichrist, and predicting with it his own martyrdom at Rome. He found many followers in both sexes, about one hundred men and three times the number of women, who, with their more tender susceptibilities and their love of romance, were an easy prey to his indiscreet zeal. Personal sympathy for a man has always been a powerful reason both for good and evil, but there exists a sure test as to its virtue, obedience to the highest authority in the Church. When these Manfredians had received the habit of

114

the Third Order of St. Dominic at his hands, they seemed to live in a state of emancipation from the rest of the Church so as to deserve the epithet of anti-christian sect which St. Antoninus of Florence bestowed upon them, and when Martin V., the Pope elected at Constance, ordered them to disperse, they gave this clear proof that their spirit came not of God, they still followed Manfred to escape from the toils of Antichrist, that is, committed grievous sin to avoid imaginary danger. Things were brought to a head by the counsel given by Bernardine's companion friar to one of the women of the sect, who asked if she might make a vow to follow Manfred without her husband's knowledge or consent. When the Saint heard of this dangerous tampering with a Divine law, he made it his business to signalize the double error which Manfred was propagating, the coming of Antichrist, and separation without mutual consent. It was to avenge these efforts that the sectarian pointed at Bernardine as an innovator and an encourager of idolatry. Did he not expose the Holy Name for adoration?

If there had not been something particularly significant in this devotion, there would have been neither trouble nor suffering in its inauguration. When the Church, like a beautiful tree or plant, begins to put forth branches and flowers which were not previously discernible to human eye, the cry is sometimes raised, 'Who has done this, the enemy has sown seed whilst we slept?' But the head gardener is called, and upon examination he finds that the new green shoot or bud is only a natural development of what is already in the tree, and he says that the branch may live and flourish. This is the history of nearly every devotion in the Church which is to have a great career, and we have instances of it in two prominent cases. Juliana of Retinne was treated as demented when she asked for the festival of Corpus Christi, and Margaret Mary suffered bitter persecution for the Sacred Heart. Bernardine has borne witness for the Holy Name.

The machinations of Manfred and his party were allowed to prevail, and Bernardine who was then preaching the Lent at Viterbo, was summoned by Martin V to Rome in order to answer the accusation of heresy. Manfred alleged against him that he was a preacher of a dangerous extravagance with the motive of drawing people after himself, and that his little tablets were idolatrous. The difference between the Saint and the fanatic appears very forcibly as a result of Martin's temporary decision. He forbade Manfred his followers, and Bernardine the instrument of his pretended idolatry. The one gave the example of complete obedience, whereas no authority had power over Manfred's will. As a more striking contrast to Bernardine's entire submission, he acted on the devil's device, *Non serviam*, and continued to wield the sceptre over his followers.

The Saint's reception by the Holy Father is a powerful comment on the text, *Vanity of vanity and all things are vanity, except serving God and Him alone.* Had Bernardine not been in the fullest acceptation of the word a chosen soul, he must have succumbed in the fire of calumny. It was the spring of 1427, consequently ten years since the decision of Constance had restored peace to the Holy City,

After twenty years spent in evangelizing Italy, Bernardine was received at Rome with every mark of rigour, and Martin V gave him severely to understand that unless the charge could be fully disproved,, he would be made an example to others. Probably all Rome was astir with the impending trial, for the Sovereign Pontiff wished to have the points discussed in his own presence in the Basilica of St. Peter. On the other side, Bernardine's spiritual relations, the Franciscans, and of these more particularly the Observants, justly looked upon his disgrace as a matter very closely affecting themselves, and in this, their zeal to defend the Saint stands out in a marked contrast to his perfect calmness. 'Leave God to act,' or 'God has a care of these things,' were his words when questioned as to the cause of his great equanimity. Without such persecutions, he would also say, his soul would have been in imminent danger of eternal death.[123] They who have experienced the bitterness of calumny will acknowledge the heroic virtue of a man possessing his soul in patience under its influence. As if contempt and unkindness had been the most natural reward of his labours, Bernardine awaited the decision which was to affect his whole subsequent career. Either he would be permitted to resume the ministry which was so much a part of his life, that he applied to himself the words of St. Paul: 'I came not to baptize, but to preach;' or he would be branded as a heretic, or at least as a rash innovator who is viewed always with suspicion by the Catholic instinct of conservatism. Whilst the sentence was pending, the Saint, whom a kind of spiritual affinity drew so near to Bernardine, comes

---

[123] *Vita*, p. 760.

before us in all the beauty of natural chivalry of character chastened and purified by grace. We speak of St. John Capistran. He, too, was a friar of the Observance, and when news reached him at Naples of Bernardine's trouble, he set out speedily to employ the powers of his eloquence in his brother's defence. With a fearless ardour he carried the banner of the Holy Name through the streets of Rome, preaching it to the multitude in the eager confidence of triumph. The step favourably impressed Martin V, and when a few days later, Bernardine stood upon his trial, it was satisfactorily proved that, not zeal for the truth, but jealousy, had inspired the opposition. The Sovereign Pontiff was now as anxious to honour the Saint as he had previously been disposed to suspicion and severity, and as with the saints personal fame or dishonour is a very small consideration, and the glory of God the all-absorbing question of their lives, to extol the devotion which he had preached with unwearied zeal would be the greatest happiness, nay, in one sense, the consummation of Bernardine's apostolate. The day following, Rome put its first seal upon explicit veneration of the Holy Name. Bernardine's own device, the word Jesus written on a sun, surrounded by a halo, was adopted as its outward expression, and the banner, already familiarized to the Romans by John Capistran's ardour, was now solemnly carried through the streets whilst Bernardine himself was invited to preach its glories in the Eternal City, where he remained for the space of eighty days. There, too, he became a successful apostle, for one who preaches a special devotion has generally a particular mission to fulfil. Love of the Holy Name was the heavenly antidote against the universal forgetfulness of God in Italy, and the vice which was a consequence of that forgetfulness.

But persecution had not said its last word against the preacher of the Holy Name. In the second year of Eugenius IV's Pontificate, 1432, precisely the same attempt to defame Bernardine was renewed by the followers of Manfred. Once more the Saint was cited to appear in Rome, but this time his enemies had reckoned without the most important person there. When Eugenius became fully aware of their machinations, he disavowed them entirely so far as he was concerned as Head of the Church. And furthermore, he published a Bull not only to clear the Saint from their calumnies, but to extol him as one of God's faithful servants.[124]

It is Bossuet's remark about our Lady and St. Joseph that from the time our Lord adopted them, as it were, for His own, their life was a cross and a martyrdom. Until the birth of our Lord they had never been without a house, but as soon as He was born, they were forced to take refuge in a stable. 'When Jesus enters into a place, He brings with Him His Cross and all His thorns, and distributes them to those whom He loves.'[125] In the first joys of her Maternity our Lady was told that her Child 'was a sign which should be contradicted,'[126] and the prophecy has received what we might call a special fulfilment in the lives of those saints who have particularly cherished the Sacred Humanity. On two separate occasions

---

124 *Chronica.*

125 *Premier Sermon sur St. Joseph.*

126 St. Luke ii. 34.

Bernardine was charged with imposture, hypocrisy, and heresy. But he possessed his soul in patience whilst under the ban of calumny, and if he finally triumphed, it was rather by what he left unsaid than by what he said. The secret of that heroic peace was his interior and silent communion with Jesus, the Lover of men and men's Beloved. What can be said of no earthly affection is true of Divine love; it feeds at once the three powers of man, memory, will, and understanding, to their full measure, whilst the heart replenishes itself from those inexhaustible fountains. St. Bernard, to whom Bernardine bore so close a resemblance, has expressed something of this in those beautiful lines:

> Jesu dulcis memoria,
> Dans vera cordi gaudia,
> Sed super mel et omnia
> Ejus dulcis praesentia.

CHAPTER IX.

Life in Death.

How much a man must love God before he can hope to be persecuted for God! How much of mortification and penance go to make up an apostle! The Kingdom of Heaven suffers violence, so do souls, and the perfection of Bernardine's inner life, as the glimpses of it which have come down to us testify, is the real key to his apostleship. When a man stirs up the hearts of multitudes and renovates, so to say, a whole generation, we may rightly infer that in private he leads the life of an angel.

In speaking of virginity our Lord uttered two sentences of apparently contrary drift. He said all men take not this word, but they to whom it is given, and again, he that can take, let him take it. In the first instance virginity is a gift, but a gift which previous goodness has the power to draw down, as the Spouse in the holy Canticle is attracted by aromatical spices. When our Lord said, *Qui potest capere, capiat,* did He not mean to point out that His call to virginity was binding upon no man's conscience, and more entirely a matter of his free will than perhaps any other grace of God? The very perfection indeed of consecration to God is the absence of any command. He expresses a wish, and blessed is the man at whose hands God seems to ask a willing sacrifice, if he gives, as he is gently-asked to give, wholly and entirely. The way in which Bernardine understood his vow of chastity is most significant. During his early years of religion it happened once, as he was begging from door to door, according to the custom of the Friars Minor, that a certain woman invited him as he passed to come in. When she had him in her power, she made known the real object of her invitation, which was to declare a guilty passion for Bernardine. The Saint stood and trembled, whilst he besought God to give him light to deal with the temptation. Then he told the woman that to satisfy her evil desires, she must bare her shoulders, but no sooner had she complied than Bernardine quietly took his discipline, and gave her such a castigation as she never forgot. Her temptation disappeared so completely that in her whole subsequent life she never again experienced the same kind of assault.[127]

At that time the Saint was at Capriola, a spot which he particularly loved and which continued to be the head-quarters of his religious life. Capriola was situated near Siena in the midst of quiet country. Originally it had been a little hermitage, which had awakened Bernardine's innate love of solitude. He had begged it from the Hospital of Santa Maria di Scala for himself and some few of his companions, thus transforming it into a small foundation of the Observance. Virginity and humility are essentially Catholic virtues. They need the food of the sacraments and the bosom of Holy Church in order to expand unto their farthest limits, and where they seem to flourish in other communities we would suggest that it is among the Catholic at heart. The great preacher in his monastery was distinguished, so to speak, only by the absence of all distinction. The voice which thundered in the pulpit against vice sank to a gentle whisper when it became necessary to correct even inferiors at home. Once a good friar asked the Saint how he should best fulfil the duties of his state, and Bernardine, with a deep prostration, merely replied, 'Down, down.' At another time when questioned on his opinions of theology which he had been practically studying during his thirty-years' ministry, he answered, 'Now I seem to under- stand it less than ever.[128]

In striking contrast with the Saint's humility was his own conviction of the reality of his mission.

---

[127] *Ex Analectis.* p. 768.
[128] *Vita*, p. 757.

On several occasions the popular voice designed him for a bishopric, and Siena in particular was anxious to possess her son as a pastor. But Bernardine would never listen to any entreaties of the kind. The habit and poverty of St. Francis were dearer to him than honour, and an active ministry was his call. If he had to choose, he said, he would rather live only five days and escape the bishopric, that free and without the episcopal responsibility he might hasten to the end of life's short day. The weight of pastoral cares was what he feared, not the labour of souls. Moreover, he added, as he was received with episcopal honours in every city which he entered, he would certainly fall in dignity if he became bishop of one. He preferred being bishop of all Italian cities.[129]

There was a rumour once that Bernardine would have been elected Archbishop of Milan but for his refusal. To those who remonstrated he replied earnestly: 'Do not think that I will change my elevated government for any episcopal dignity whatever.' The Saint alluded this time to the Observance whereof he had been chosen Vicar in 1438. He and his friend St. John Capistran were the two olive trees of this Reform which repaired the falling house of St. Francis.[130] In 1441 John succeeded him as its Vicar and inherited all and perhaps something more than his spiritual guide's own ardour for the work. At the time of Bernardine's admission to the Order, one hundred and thirty friars had been the whole number of

---

[129] II *Vita*, p. 757.

[130] "Qui Francisci eversam fere domum erexerunt" (*In Comment.* 721).

Observants in Italy; at his death they numbered over four thousand.[131] But however great this work may have been, and it was both great and important as a wide movement towards moral reformation, Bernardine's own ministry seems to have eclipsed it. Cardinal Gabriel, afterwards Eugenius IV, fearing that in the end the Saint might yield to the constant efforts which were made to lay upon him the pastoral charge, sent him privately a person of confidence, begging him not thus to forego the fruit of his labours. But Bernardine clasping the messenger's hand answered: 'I give you my word that I will never be guilty of the folly of yielding. Go and tell him (the Cardinal) what I say. Ask him to be quite at ease in what concerns me on this head.'[132]

One day when the question of his becoming Bishop of Siena was mooted for the first time, Bernardine called to him a very illiterate lay-brother, who was remarkable also for his purity of life and therefore dear to the Saint, and began with him a conversation after the fashion of St. Philip's *e poi*.

'I have got something to tell you, dear Brother, which will be a source of lasting joy to us. The Sienese have unanimously chosen me as their Bishop. Is not this excellent news?'

'O Father,' was the answer, 'do not lose the fruit of so much labour in teaching the people, for a passing good.'

---

131 *Analecta*, p. 768.
132 *Vita Maphaei*, etc., p. 758.

'What then if the Milanese, by whom I am most loved and honoured, should wish me to be their Archbishop, would you make little of this too?'

'Truly, being a higher place, I say you ought to shun it with greater zest unless you would condemn yourself and all subsequent preachers of the truth to shame.'

'And what,' asked Bernardine again, 'if the Sovereign Pontiff should make me a Patriarch, would you tell me that I should not willingly accept the dignity?'

'Now,' cried the Brother in sorrow, 'I see that you have been captivated by the vain things of this world which will make you lose the grace of God and the love of souls whom you had sought out with so much zeal.'

'What if I become a Cardinal, do you think I ought to look down upon this honour too?'

'Here too, Father, there is little to be said, for who could not easily be enslaved by so high a dignity? Put an end to my suspense, Father, do what you mean to do.'

But the Saint saw the good Brother had heard enough of his supposed schemes, and ended by saying 'that the most eminent positions were also the most perilous and the most to be despised. For his part he would not exchange the habit of St. Francis for any high place whatsoever, no, not even for the Papacy.'[133]

But Bernardine's beautiful life was drawing to a close; old in years, he was young in spirit with something of the vigour of eternity, because his treasure was centred upon that which the saints love in Heaven. 'Having loved His own, He loved them unto the end,' St. John tells us of the Sacred Heart. The same was true in a proportionate degree of Bernardine of Siena. There is no sign of weakness or decay about his end, and it was his glory to die at last in full armour, as an earthly warrior might lay himself down to sleep after the battle with all the tokens of the fight around him. His biographers have closely followed him in his last months, when, they say, like the dying swan, he sang most sweetly.

It will be remembered that the Saint had spent his very early years at Massa, and in consideration; of the temporal life he had received in that city, it was one of the last places to call forth his apostolic zeal. There he preached the Lent of 1444, and one of those miracles into which he put so much of himself, if we may use the term, is recorded of him. Saints are characterized by their particular modes of working miracles. One day then after his sermon, a poor leper, a Spaniard by birth, approached Bernardine and begged him for some shoes to ease his tormented feet. Not having wherewith to give alms, the apostle took off his own sandals, and bestowed them upon the man. The leper went his way, but the sandals consecrated by so many steps in the work of saving souls, proved stronger than the disease. The leprosy peeled off in

---

[133] *Vita*, p. 758.

scales of dry flesh, and the man found himself perfectly cured. He did not neglect the duty of gratitude, but returned to Massa to thank the master of the sandals. All that Bernardine stipulated for was silence. However, says the Spanish Chronicle, the closed mouths of his sores spoke louder than his tongue.[134] In those days, as in the days of our Lord, the cure of a leper could not fail to be an event.

Bernardine's next halting-place was Siena. The Sienese indeed hoped that he would take up his last abode amongst them, as they were disposed to claim a natural relationship to Bernardine. The Saint however had far other thoughts, and was more than ever eager only for the interests of souls. At Spoleto the civil and ecclesiastical authorities received him with great honours, justifying to the last his half-earnest, half-playful remark that it was better to be Pope in every Italian city than Bishop in one. A woman there who had been paralyzed for six years was cured by Bernardine at the invocation of the Holy Name. Leaving Umbria he arrived at Rieti, where another triumphal reception awaited him. The people of Rieti seem to have deserved the commendations of the Saint who was so soon to die, for he gave them special praise as the children of his heart. A young girl was suffering from ulcers in the breast, the disease was declared absolutely hopeless, whilst fear of speedy mortification placed her life in imminent danger. At the Governor's request, the Saint read a portion of the Gospel of St. John over

---

[134] "Las cerrades bocas de sus llagas fueran mas parleres que su lengua." (p. 506).

the patient, and bade her parents be of good cheer, for their child would live. Probably Bernardine prayed at the same time that the fame of her cure might not be attributed to him, for it was only the next day when he had left the place, that the sickness entirely disappeared.

Just a week before the end, it being the Thursday preceding the Ascension, he arrived at *Falacrina*. There he preached his last sermon, and never, as it seemed to his auditors, had his words been at once more eloquent or more earnest. At that very time his body was so weighed down by mortal sickness that his capability of travelling was in itself alone a triumph of the higher over the lower nature. He was anxious to move on, for at Aquila, as his more than human knowledge told him, he would enter into the joy of his Lord. On the Saturday, whilst travelling on his ass, being overcome with thirst and fatigue, he asked his companions to help him to dismount and to get him a little water. The place was very dry, but a peasant who happened, to pass, guided them to a spring. When our Lord had partaken of the Last Supper, He told His disciples that He should not again taste wine till He came to His Father's Kingdom. [135] Before that fountain in the cool and shady nook where no sound could be heard excepting the play of its waters, Bernardine rested for a while, and he too might have said that it was for the last time. For him there was to be no more halting-place, but yet a few days, and endless joy and rest with God. The gentle murmuring of the fountain seemed to him like a *Sursum corda*; begging his companions to leave him to his solitude, he became rapt in God. He had

---

[135] St. Matt. xxvi. 29.

a vision of St. Peter Celestine, who foretold to him that they should share the patronage of Aquila.

On Sunday he arrived in a dying state at the city where he was to leave his earthly covering. A popular and turbulent insurrection had broken out against the nobility, but this, which meant good to be done, only served as a further enticement to the apostle of Italy. He found not peace but the sword, yet when his bodily voice had become forever silent, his very death spoke peace. The Fathers of the Observance had no house in Aquila itself, and it was judged expedient to receive Bernardine in the monastery of the Conventuals as offering by its position more convenience for his treatment. A writer of our own time[136] mentions what would be a significant coincidence if it could be fully proved. The dying Bernardine, he says, was lodged in the cell of an absent friar, no other than St. John Capistran, who inherited the spirit and labours of the Apostle of Italy, as Bernardine had succeeded to the Apostle of the Judgment. But St. John was an Observant, and we do not see how he could have had a regular home in the monastery of Conventuals.

Aquila, in spite of its civil strife, resolved to send a deputation to Bernardine, for although the Saint declared he had come there to labour for the peace, and the prevention of those scandals which he had so often signalized, it soon became known that he was dying. After his death his words appear to have been answered in a most singular manner, as indeed the prayers of God's faithful servants

---

[136] Malou. *Vie de Ste. Catherine de Sienne.*

alone are answered. 'O my children,' he exclaimed with his own vigorous fervour, 'I admonish you to peace and harmony. My God, if I could buy this peace with my blood, how willingly I would offer the sacrifice to prevent scandals so pernicious, and put out the fire of vengeance with the blood of my veins. Receive, Lord, my desire, and if my blood can be accepted for peace, there is yet time. I make this offering with all my heart to Thy greater honour and glory.'[137]

In the meantime death brooked no further delay. The Saint called his confessor, Fra Bartolomeo of Siena, received the last sacraments of Holy Church, and begged that when his hour came, he might be placed upon ashes on the floor. On the evening of the 20th of May 1444, whilst the Friars were chanting in Choir the verse, *Pater, manifestavi Nomen Tuum hominibus*, the lover and apostle of the Holy Name of Jesus passed away.

The miracles which followed this blessed death are no exception in the lives of the saints. Without delay God publicly answered the petition which His servant had offered up on this side of the grave. After the ceremony of the funeral had been performed in the Cathedral, the holy corpse was carried back to the Franciscan church, and there exposed uncovered in a coffin in a chapel for the unusual time of twenty-six days. [138] Placid and beautiful, Bernardine lay there in death, his body diffusing that particular fragrance which is known as the odour of sanctity, whilst the Italian cities, where

---

[137] *Chronica*, p. 514.
[138] *Analecta*, p. 774.

he had preached, celebrated demonstrations in honour of their departed apostle. But all was not peace yet in Aquila. Whilst the body of St. Bernardine still awaited burial, the party-spirit rose to so great a pitch that the different factions had recourse to arms, and the ungovernable enmity produced strife on both sides. The clergy and magistracy vainly interposed, when a voice in the air was distinctly heard to say: 'Put down your arms: if you wish for blood, you will find wherewith to quench your thirst in the convent of St. Francis.' The Bishop mindful of the prodigies recently worked by St. Bernardine, led off the conflicting parties in something like triumph to the spot named, and there indeed they found streams of blood flowing from the nostrils of the dead Saint. At the sight of the miracle the combatants forgot their enmity: in death they felt that St. Bernardine's heart was still amongst them, and that the prayer of his failing lips: 'My God, how willingly I would put out the fire of vengeance with the blood of my veins,' had not been uttered in vain.

Surely we may claim for him a foremost place amongst the lovers of Italy. Others have sought for it intellectual fame, and advanced civilization, or have crowned it Queen of the Muses. Many of its children have sighed for its unity through the twilight of its slowly developed political history. Yet Bernardine surpassed all these patriots in proportion as the object of his labours was higher and nobler. Zeal for souls inspired the purest of sacrifices, life-long combats, self-forgetfulness carried to its utmost limits. Who, indeed, loved Italy best? *Dulce et decorum est pro patria mori* has more than its equivalent in the language of the Gospel:

131

'Greater love than this no man hath that he giveth his life for his friend.'

III.

ST. JOHN CAPISTRAN.

1385— 1456.

CHAPTER X.

The Kingdom of Heaven suffering violence.

It is a question which admits of a variety of judgments amongst Catholics whether God shows greater love for a soul when He causes it to be born in the true faith, or when He seeks it out in the darkness of heresy and brings it to the knowledge of Himself as the true Light. The same sort of question applies to vocations. Is it more blessed for the soul by, as it were, a spontaneous and uniform growth of holiness, which is itself the gift of God, to make choice of Him, or to be singled out as the object of a special predilection by His breaking in with loving violence upon a course of previous indifference or worldiness?

St. Vincent Ferrer and St. Bernardine of Siena were both marked with their vocation from their earliest years of reason, but St. John Capistran was one of those to whom God vouchsafed to do violence. His natural character made him a hero, his correspondence with unusual grace made him a saint. Chivalry, generosity, honour, devotion to one's sovereign, may be accounted as human virtues, and of them, when they form part of nature, our Lord has said: 'Amen, I say unto you, they have received their reward.' Other virtues bear about them a look so unmistakeably supernatural that they must be acknowledged to be the fruits of a doctrine which is not of this world. There never indeed existed a man to whom mortification and self-humiliation came naturally, nor was there ever a saint who did not make these two virtues his special study. Before his conversion a fine sense of honour seems to have been not only the salient feature in St. John's character, but also a quality which prepared his soul for better things. And in after years, true to his chivalrous nature, the same integrity stands out though transformed and perfected by the Christian spirit. His character, then, could no longer be expressed in the words, 'he was the soul of honour,' but his whole working is brought out in those other words, 'he loved justice and hated iniquity.'

John had been the friend and active companion of Bernardine of Siena for some years, and besides being a brother in religion, he always looked upon that Saint as his master in the spiritual life, propagating with all his zeal Bernardine's favourite devotion to the Holy Name, and often applying a relic of his friend as a shelter to his own humility in order to obtain miraculous cures. We cannot adopt the notion that Bernardine struck down at last on the road-side, so to say, by mortal sickness, departed to God in St. John's cell at Aquila, but it is certain that the disciple carried on his master's ministry to souls, and became a great apostle and wonder-worker to his generation. Bernardine had been the special Apostle of Italy: John was in general the Apostle of Peace.

It is evident that the word apostleship implies either that there is something to impart or something to renovate; an apostle builds up or he restores that which has fallen into decay. When a call is given by God -publicly to preach peace, we, generally speaking, surmise that the world is in a very unsatisfactory state. War and strife are the very contrary to that legacy bequeathed by our Lord in so marked a way by the words so often repeated:

'My peace I leave unto you, My peace I give unto you.' Peace implies charity, and charity is the whole of the law and the prophets. *Pax* was the motto of the first western monks, the Benedictines, when the world appeared to them so bad that leaving it altogether seemed to them the fittest way to benefit it. What did St. John's peace mean? It signified, perhaps, that there was strife where the bond of Catholic charity should have united all hearts. In the Church itself there was a falling away from piety and goodness, and the poet's *auri sacra fames* had entered into holy places. The great point to bear in mind is that a man's or even an age's wickedness is powerless to affect dogma. Men pass away and God's truth abides for ever, whether it is propagated by the good or by the bad. Almighty God punishes sins in the Church in His own way, sometimes by a spiritual chastisement, sometimes by temporal suffering, or by both. The reformation worked by St. Vincent's preaching had conduced to the peace of Constance, and the vigour of St. John Capistran dealt an energetic blow upon the power of the Turk. The taking of Constantinople and the Ottoman invasion appear in the light of a second Divine admonition that punishment would fall upon the Church unless there was a thorough reformation of morals, and half a century later the premonitory symptoms of Divine wrath were followed by the advent of Luther.

The troubled state of the Kingdom of Naples at that time goes to prove how far even in the realm which formed less than one-third of her territory Italy was removed from unity. The House of Anjou had been reigning since 1266, and in 1343, Joanna I, as granddaughter of Robert the

137

Wise, succeeded to the throne. Her reign is a dark tragedy, enacted to the sound of music and revelry. To support a sovereign of her kind without sustaining shocks, the monarchical principle would have needed to be firmly engrafted upon national life and customs in her kingdom. 'A bad sovereign,' says a great upholder of monarchy,[139] 'is like a hailstorm falling from above, which one must bear.' But the Neapolitans had not arrived at that forbearance of individuals for the principle's sake, and when Joanna had run out her best years in appalling licentiousness, it became necessary to think of her successor. The dissensions arising from various claims cost the kingdom two years of active strife. The Queen had married her only sister, Mary, to Charles de Duras, who became later Carlo della Pace. This same Charles was perhaps not a little aggrieved when Joanna invited over as her heir Louis of Anjou, son of the French King, thus adding to the complications at home, and preparing two whole centuries of trouble for her country.[140] But the step cost her death, for Charles caused her to be strangled, and succeeded her himself in 1381. In this state of affairs it becomes easy to realize the enormous evil of the Papal schism even in a temporal sense. If the true Pope favoured one party, the anti-Pope was quite sure to uphold the opponent whoever he might be, and it was easy for a bad sovereign to change his allegiance as it suited his fortunes. Thus all notion of right was gradually weakened. Carlo della Pace did not long enjoy his ill-gotten diadem. He succumbed in 1386 to a plot in Hungary, and was succeeded by his son,

---

[139] Joseph de Maistre, *Lettres et Opuscules inédits.*
[140] Cantix, Histoire des Italiens, t. vi. p. 268.

Ladislaus. We have made this digression because the fortunes of John Capistran were intimately connected with the son of Carlo della Pace. Ladislaus himself had little thought beyond his personal ambition. He sinned away his life, dreaming vaguely of united Italy. He marched upon the Papal Patrimony, and took the title of its King with 'Caesar or nobody'[141] as his device.

According to the most accurate account,[142] John Capistran's father was a German, who followed Charles de Duras from Verona to Italy, and Ladislaus rewarded the father's fidelity by showing favour to his son. The Saint was born at Capistran, a city of Lower Abruzzo, on the 24th of June, 1385 or 1386, for there is some uncertainty as to the exact date. His parents were both noble, but John could never have known his father, who died whilst he was quite an infant. No special incident is preserved to us of his early years, though perhaps this lack is only in keeping with the peculiar call which was to be his later on. We are told of his singular capacity for learning as a child, and after the completion of his earlier education, he was sent to Perugia, where legal studies were particularly flourishing. There he passed ten whole years under the guidance of the then celebrated Peter Ubaldo, and himself acquired no meagre fame as a lawyer. Ten years out of the spring of life devoted to secular pursuits, without apparently any of that interior spirit which ennobles for God the commonest occupation, did nevertheless prepare perfection in

---

141 Cantù, Storia Universale, vol. vii. p. 386.

142 That of the Bollandists, *Commentarius Praevius in Vitam Sti. Johannis Capistrani*, p. 273.

the future preacher. Those talents which caused him to be sought out in the world he afterwards turned to gold for the profit of eternal souls. Perugia would naturally have acknowledged the temporal dominion of the Pope, but at that time, in consequence of a treaty between John XXIII and Ladislaus,[143] it was under the authority of the King of Naples. In the year 1424, it returned once more into the possession of the Sovereign Pontiff, then Martin V. Probably one of the best things King Ladislaus ever did was to appoint John Capistran Vicar of the Perugian Republic. Though in the very flower of his years, he had arrived at a maturity of mind and judgment so remarkable that no one could be astonished at the King's choice; and in 1412, he entered, at the age of twenty-six, on his new functions in the city, which he no doubt viewed as his Alma Mater. During his administration, we have a striking example of fidelity to the monarchical authority, however bad the representatives of that authority might be. It once happened that Ladislaus caused a certain count and his son to be arrested on the charge of treason. John was amongst the judges. The trial proved the guilt of the father, but the innocence of the son. When the King heard this verdict, he ordered the beheading of the Count, and that a sham sentence of death should be passed upon the son, who after having witnessed his father's execution should be set

---

[143] 'Sub hoc anno (1412) die xv. Junii inter Joannem XXIII et Ladislaum Neapolitanum compositum foedus fuit, quo inter alias factiones Ladislao oppignorabantur civitates Asculum, Viterbium, Penisia, Beneventum, donee ipsi Joannes XXIII. solveret ducenta ac viginti aureorum millia'(Comment. Prav. p. 275).

at liberty. The consequence of this cruel sentence answered to the probable anticipations of Ladislaus. Fear at the sight of his father's torment caused the son's death. John was struck with remorse for having been a party to the sentence, and one writer traces his religious calling to it; but although a determination of the kind would have been quite in keeping with his character, he did not actually leave the world till 1416. Grace may have tried to speak to his heart, though the time for his total conversion had not arrived. Ladislaus died in 1414, at the age of thirty-six, prematurely worn out by vice and licentiousness, and his sister, Joanna II, who succeeded to the throne, scarcely differed in her bearing and tastes from her namesake of sullied memory. If then John served profligate masters, his merits as a lover of honour and justice were the greater. It requires no small amount of courage to be constantly and thoroughly true even to the strongest convictions. A wealthy and powerful man offered the Governor upon one occasion a large sum of money to condemn to death a certain man, an enemy of his, already arraigned, threatening John himself with violence should he act otherwise. But the Saint, having regard to truth and justice alone, pronounced the man entirely innocent. It was one of the evil customs of those times to put criminals who had not owned their guilt to the torture, and naturally it often happened that pain extorted false confession. John strove to remedy this, and to do so he had recourse to an ingenious stratagem. Going to the stables, he openly took away his horse's saddle, and carefully hid it. Then calling his groom, he enjoined him to get the horse ready for him, but of course the saddle could not be found. John laid the theft to the groom's charge, and had him tortured. Under pressure, the poor man called out that he had hidden it away in a certain place. Search was made, and the saddle not being found, the torture was once more applied. The second time an entirely new version was extracted from the groom, who said he had sold it for a sum of money. After this rough experience, he resolved never again to have recourse to so depraved a means of finding out, not the truth indeed, but falsehood.[144]

These two incidents give the notion of a strong and upright character. John's administration was so perfect as to order and justice, and in this particular he was far beyond his time, that throughout his small domain security and freedom belonged even to the traveller who 'carried gold in his hand.'[145] He was charitable to the poor, both with money and with kind words. But these virtues were natural to him, or perhaps they were strengthened by prosperity, for it is peculiar to a noble nature not to grow hard or insolent when the sun of this world is shining on it, but kind and tender, and in proportion as it enjoys temporal blessings to be anxious that others less favoured should partake of them. Perhaps this effect of riches on a man is the very best test of his goodness. And John was prosperous. He held the royal favour, a post of high honour, and was probably wealthy in proportion. The sweets of human affection were not to be wanting. From what afterwards occurred, we gather that his marriage must have taken place towards the end of his governorship, in 1416. The

---

144 Comment. Praev. p. 276.
145 Vita auctore Christophoro a Varisio, p. 492.

bride of his choice was a rich heiress of Perugia, but in the midst of so much happiness and natural goodness, we are told that he was entirely given up to the things of this world. His awakening came to him in the usual shape, by suffering. He expresses in his own words something of the vanity and pride of that position from which the transition to a prison was so rapid. Long years afterwards, as John gave the habit of the third order to a certain man and his wife, he made a confession of a secret vanity in dressing of his hair. 'In the year 1416, I was to return into my country, Capistran, to claim the inheritance which was necessary to me on my marriage, though I had taken my degree, and was about thirty years old. . . . Every man called me Don John, and amongst other things, I took a great pride in my hair, which was streaked with gold, and curled according to the fashion of my country.'[146] The popular Governor was to be sacrificed to one of those sudden revulsions of feeling, only possible when a country is divided between contesting factions. The Perugian Republic was troubled at that time by the dissensions of the Malatestas and the Rimini on the one side, and the Bracchi on the other. John, as the faithful servant of Queen Joanna II, incurred the anger of both, and was at length put into prison at Brufa by the Perugians, who thought they had secured a grand prize. He was lodged in a tower, loaded with heavy chains, and given nothing but a little bread and water wherewith to sustain life. Solitude proves a man, but John's efforts in his first imprisonment seem to have been directed towards effecting his escape. When he had been for some months in the tower, he began to form his

---

[146] Comment. Praev. p. 277

plans. He took the blanket or covering from his bed, and tore it up, together with his cloak, into strips with his teeth, failing a knife, and having applied this improvised rope to the Avail, he began to descend as best he could. But in God's designs, prison had not accomplished its work yet, and John sprained his foot in letting himself down, and could not get on. The noise of his chains attracted one of the keepers of the tower, so that thinking to avoid Charybdis he fell upon Scylla. He was thrown into a most miserable dungeon, so damp that he found himself knee deep in water, while an iron chain, bound round his middle, kept him in a standing position. His food consisted as before in a wretched pittance of bread and water. At the end of three days, he fell asleep from sheer fatigue, or, as other biographers say, he was reciting, according to his daily custom, the Office of the Immaculate Conception, when a light, as if from Heaven suddenly filled the dungeon, and he saw in the air the figure of a Friar Minor with the stigmata on his hands and feet, who addressed him in these words:

'What art thou doing? Why dost thou wait? What dost thou expect? Obey the voice of God, and follow His bidding'

And John, fearing, as it were, to hear the answer of the heavenly messenger, temblingly asked, 'What would God have me do?'

'Dost thou not understand what He has decreed to do with thee?' said the friar. 'Seest thou the habit which I wear? Thou too must put it on, and leave the world which has proved itself so fallacious.'

But John received this answer in great sadness, for 'It is a hard saying,' he murmured; 'to live in a cloister, and to give up liberty forever. Such a thought had never occurred to me, but if God commands I will obey.'[147] Here was the beginning of fidelity, and a very meritorious fidelity, an illuminated mind with a dry heart; for in a vocation as in a conversion, the first leap must often be taken in the dark. This was, however, no more than a half resolution, because he could hardly help himself under the pressure of a heavenly visitor. When St. Francis (for it was he) had disappeared, it may be inferred that John wished to hear no more of this extraordinary calling. But the surrender of his cherished hair was to be the knife of sacrifice. Once more he fell asleep without any particular thought of religion, and when he awoke, the fine curls of auburn hair were no more to be seen. An invisible hand had shaved him after the Franciscan fashion, that is, his head was shaven so as to leave him nothing but a crown of hair. In educating a man's higher nature, how much suffering Almighty God may cause the lower to suffer! The object of this Divine violence by no means submitted with a good grace to be thus torn away from the worldly vanities, figured under those locks of hair. At first he burst out indignantly, 'Feeling no attraction to religion, I am astonished at Thee, Almighty God, for striving to make me a religious against my will.'[148]

---

[147] Comment. Praev. p. 279.

[148] 'Quum nullum affectum ad religioncm habeam, miror de Te Omnipotens Deus, quod me invitum religiosum facere proponas.'

145

Then at last he acknowledged that it availed but little to kick against the goad, he could no longer find enjoyment in his former life, except at the price of stifling Divine inspirations, so he yielded to the action of the Holy Spirit, and began to experience 'the peace which surpasseth all understanding.' They who put their hands to the plough are admonished not to look backwards, but to their work, and during John's long apostolate no moment of weakness or faint-heartedness is recorded of him. The winter was really over and gone after that last episode in the dungeon. The flowers of the highest virtues soon began to appear; the man of the world had put on the armour of Christian knighthood.

He besought his gaolers to procure for him some brown stuff, such as the Friars Minor wear, with scissors, needle, and thread, for since a prisoner might not be formally clothed with the habit of religion, he was going to try to manufacture one for himself. It is said his keepers loved him so much for his endearing qualities, that they sent for the things -required for this novel tailoring, but those who had imprisoned him, when they heard of his desire, uttered some such words as these: 'We know his bad ways, and don't let him think to deceive us by such tricks, or imagine that he is going to escape. We will tighten his chains and augment the number of his gaolers, and then see if he succeeds in taking himself off.' [149] But by the presence of the cross, humiliation, and derision, John was not daunted. He knew, he said, that in resolving to become a Friar Minor, he gave up his

---

[149] Comment, p. 280.

will both in pleasant and unpleasant things; and when he was roughly asked why he sought to deceive by the religious habit, he answered with perfect truth, 'I do not deceive you, nor has it ever been my custom to act with dishonesty, but rather with sincerity in everything.'[150] At length a Friar Minor of the Observance, who enjoyed a reputation of great sanctity, was allowed to come to John's cell to see what sort of vocation he had received. When first he distinguished the prisoner in the brown habit of his Order, he smilingly said, 'Well, Lord John, what kind of habit have you got there?' But after Lord John 'had poured out the history of his strange call, he smiled no longer, but gravely summed up his judgment by saying that the finger of God was in the sudden change. So sure was the holy friar of this that he offered to stay as a hostage in the captive's place till negotiations respecting his liberty could be carried out. However he succeeded in impressing John's keepers, and they allowed him to go free in virtue of a ransom of 400 ducats, which, if calculated at their corresponding value in the present day, would amount to no less than 160,000 francs,[151] a ransom which by its amount indicates the high rank of the prisoner. When the Saint appeared again in Perugia he was joyfully greeted by his old friends with many inquiries as to how he had escaped from his enemies' hands, but for John there was no longer any relish in his old life or familiar ties. He burned to spread that Divine fire which the Son of God has enkindled upon the earth, and he hastened to put his affairs in order that there might be no delay. But here a difficulty

---

[150] Vita a Varisio, p. 493.
[151] Comment, pp. 278, 280.

will occur to the mind of the reader. He had married a wife, and moreover she opposed his step. The very fact that John did not yield to her opposition proves (what in a question of this kind is a determining point) that the marriage had not been followed by their living together. If it had been otherwise, John would have been bound to listen to her objections. As it was, she ended by promising to enter religion, but broke her promise by marrying twice. He, on his side, returned the marriage portion.[152]

It is said that during the whole course of his subsequent life, no razor was ever needed to renew the religious tonsure effected by the invisible hand. But even that wonder belonged to a lesser order than the sudden transformation of a rich and worldly man into a poor and humble son of Francis.

CHAPTER XL

The Royal Way of the Holy Cross.

John, indeed, belonged to that race of men who cannot do things by halves. When he had sold his worldly possessions and distributed them to the poor, he sought out the Guardian of the Friars Minor of the Observance, whose monastery was situated in the neighbourhood of Perugia. Neither sweet words nor hearty welcome awaited him there, for the Fathers, and especially the Guardian, a

---

[152] Pp. 280. 443.

shrewd as well as a highly spiritual man, wanted to ascertain whether the new postulant was made of 'clay or silver.'[153] Riches and a lofty station do not of themselves lead to a religious vocation, nor does authority, naturally speaking, produce a taste for obedience. So when John had disclosed his wish, the Guardian roughly replied to this effect: that their monastery was not a refuge for vanity or a lost reputation, nor a resource for disappointed men, but a school of virtues, and a place of retirement for the truly poor in spirit. A man who had given up his best years to enjoyment and pleasure was no fitting companion for the servants of Christ; in such a case the traces of his past life would with difficulty be effaced by the most rigid observances of religion; in fine, he, the Guardian, knew what he was about far too well to receive so great a worldling without a public renunciation of his former career. The language was hard, if it be remembered that John at worst had been merely a worldly man whose conduct had always exceeded his profession ; but under the action of the same fire, the chaff is consumed whilst the gold is purified. Except in religious houses, public humiliations have disappeared from our society, and it is difficult to realize John's acceptance of the Guardian's *onus probandi*. To prove the sincerity of his wish, he was invited to parade the streets of Perugia, a town where he had held the first rank so lately, on an ass with his face towards the tail, a cord tied round his neck, and a paper head-gear or sort of mitre, on which he was to write in legible characters, as the inflexible Guardian stated, the blackest sins of his thirty years. Even in those days a similar penance

---

153 An luteus vel argenteus sit.

could not be performed with impunity, though John never shrank from the trial. There was a general run to the windows in the streets through which the ignoble donkey passed, a cry of 'Poor man, he is crazy!' and not the least the jeerings of the little boys, who, as the Spanish chronicle truly and quaintly remarks, 'are very punctual on these occasions.'[154] Now that God had spoken to his heart, no trial or humiliation was too great for the ex-Governor. After going through this test, fierce to human nature and scorching to a nobleman, the Friars, as may be surmised, could no longer make a difficulty about receiving him, yet to try him still further, they seemed to do it with the worst possible grace. John at length took the habit on the 4th of October, 1416, at the age of thirty, and during his novitiate he tasted still more of the ignominy of the Cross. If he ever experienced a temptation to rebellion, the instances of his wife must have added fuel to the flame. She presented herself at the monastery, and besought him to give up the struggle and return to comfort. On his side he constantly spoke to her of the religious life, which she at length promised to adopt. But according to the 'fashion of women,'[155] says the biographer, she broke her word, married, and became afflicted with leprosy, which had been the punishment predicted to her by John in the event of unfaithfulness.

The novice was given up to the by no means tender mercies of a lay-brother, who acted towards him the part of special monitor, for his greater perfection and mortification. It is said that the lay-

---

[154] Chronica, quinta parte, p. 19
[155] More muliebri.

brother could not destroy John's reputation in the outer world for ability, nor prevent people from coming for his advice in urgent matters, but after these interviews he had his revenge upon vainglory. He would reproach John in these words: 'You proud man, now you fancy you are somebody. Why did you not remain in the world, if you wished to follow such vanities?'[156] On one occasion when John was ill in bed with fever, the inexorable brother brought him a scalding drink and bade him take it. The sick novice did not even protest, but calmly swallowed the draught, though, as he afterwards owned, 'I thought it would have consumed my tongue and my throat' God rewarded his blind obedience, for he got up on the instant out of bed, perfectly cured. Once when the novices were engaged in washing some cloths, the water was so boiling hot that no one ventured to commence operations. The said lay-brother, taking one of them as best he could, hurled it at John, accusing him of sloth and want of readiness. He fell on his knees to acquiesce in the judgment, the pain being so great that he thought he had lost his sight. Again no bodily harm, but great profit in the spiritual sense, came to him from the very questionable humiliation. Whether the Fathers, like the women who watched him parading his ass through the streets of Perugia, really thought him deficient, or whether they feigned it, is not quite clear. Twice, however, they dismissed him as one insane and of weak intellect, as if his conduct had not already proved him wise with the sublime folly of the Cross! These delays could not have been important, for he was professed in October, 1417.

---

[156] *Vita*, p. 495.

According to a wise custom in religious houses, the newly-fledged wings were not immediately required to fly. After his profession, John studied theology under St. Bernardine, and received Holy Orders. Thus the beginning of his active ministry may be placed about 1420. His biographers are silent as to his personal appearance, though later he is described as a little man, made up of skin, nerve, and bone, with an energy out of all proportion with his apparent strength.[157] If he was small and of no reputation, he had on the other hand an indomitable will, a power of love and of hatred which is a weapon in itself. In a word, beneath that insignificant exterior there was one of those generous souls which govern the world.[158] The code of such government is mortification, its crown self-annihilation. Its foundation is often laid on fidelity to one great grace, under a circumstance predestined by God to be the turning-point of a whole life.

St. John's ministry spread over a wide period of thirty-six years, and though his labours were chiefly expended on Italy, his biographers have laid greater stress upon his Work in Germany. His mode of life was one which would have seemed to leave nature entirely without breathing-time. He kept most rigorously, the three fasts of St. Francis, the third being left to the discretion of the Friars, and never ate meat except in his decline of strength, and even then his brethren were obliged to solicit an order from the Sovereign Pontiff. Lovers of God

---

[157] Comment, p. 283.

[158] 'Une âme généreuse dans un pauvre petit corps est la maitresse du monde.' (Lacordaire,Lettres á des Jeunes Gens).

meet, indeed, on common ground; they feed upon the self-same aspirations and sacrifices, varied only by the personal character of the sacrificer. John Capistran reproduced Vincent Ferrer's daily order of life, but there was something characteristic about John's miracles, a chivalry moulded into a most graceful humility. No sooner had St. Bernardine entered into glory, than John took advantage of his friend's sanctity to hide his own. He carried with him constantly a small biretta which had belonged to Bernardine, and some linen stained with the miraculous flow of blood after death, and it was his custom to attribute the miracles he himself wrought to his friend's virtue and intercession with God. In Germany, where he was not known except by fame, his self-forgetfulness had special merit, and one who writes about John's German mission gives a particular prominence to Bernardine's biretta in his daily life. Rising before the light, he recited Matins, Lauds, Prime, and Tierce, and then celebrated Holy Mass. After Mass he preached his sermon, using in Germany the Latin tongue, which an interpreter translated to the people. There the learned language in the pulpit seems not to have interfered in the slightest degree with the fruits of John's ministry. We need not suppose that it was on occasions when the interpreter was used that the apostle preached, as he is said to have done, for the space of four and five hours in an open place, and his audience numbered thousands. He inherited in this particular the authority of his lineage. Not merely in his speech was he an apostle, the very sight of him was often sufficient to do his Master's work. The sermon over, he retired where possible to his monastery, recited Sext and None, and imposed hands upon the sick, and after Bernardine's death, the cherished biretta. Then he took his single meal, received all who wished to see him, said Vespers, and again visited the sick. Usually he did not seek his short rest without consulting Holy Scripture, in which he was remarkably proficient. The repose which he allowed himself lasted three or four hours, and he slept in his clothes. At cock-crow he wept over his sins with St. Peter, and sunrise brought him a recollection of St. Mary Magdalen going to seek our Lord at the Sepulchre.

As to his local labours, a very broad outline only can be given. He opened his apostolic career at Siena in 1420, and, except for extraordinary missions, continued to evangelize Italy up to the year 1451, when his reputation had so wide a renown that the Emperor Frederick III invited him to Germany. He preached in Carinthia, Styria, Moravia, Thuringia, Saxony, Bohemia, and Poland, everywhere working those notable changes which mark the apostle. Like a nation, every age has its failings and its propensities, its dark and its light sides. In these days, if a St. John Capistran passed through England he would have less to say against the Methodists, Wesleyans, or Baptists, for instance, than against the spirit of infidelity which is making incursions into the mainland of revealed religion. Now the question is to believe or not to believe, then it was one of far greater detail. Instead of the infidelity of this century, men laboured for novelty in religion. They did not yet wish to throw off Revelation, but they did desire to be their own masters, and to settle their own creed. The Councils of Pisa and Bale were the outward expressions of a radicalism in faith which revolted at Catholic rule. They would have placed the governing power rather in the body than in the head, and thus their efforts were necessarily abortive. About the same time, in different parts of the world, Huss, Wycliffe, and the Fraticelli strove to propagate these errors. In the Church's realm they were the Radicals and the Fenians who were trying to overturn the house by undermining its foundation, under pretext of whitewashing its walls. It is clear, then, what the particular line of Catholic apostleship would be at such a time. It would attach itself to the conversion of individual hearts by reflecting, as if from a mirror, a high standard of the Catholic life. Like Shakespeare's hero, Hamlet, the spiritual arena, when sounded as to its thoughts, sent back the echo, 'Words, words, words.' John of Capistran's work was one of action, one of deeds opposed to empty dissertations, which never yet moved a soul to the love of eternal things. Whilst the three bishops and fourteen abbots at Bale decreed the pre-eminence of a Council over the Pope, John stirred up whole populations to moral reformation. He came, too, with his device ; and just as Vincent had said 'Penance,' Bernardine 'Jesus,' so now John said 'Peace.'

He traversed Italy from the Alps to Sicily, that is, in its entirety, and amongst the towns to which his visit is recorded are Verona in 1427, Ferrara and Trent in 1438, Capistran and Aquila in 1447, Bergamo and Vicenza in 1451, before starting to carry his peaceful ministry to Germany.

It has been seen how vigorously Bernardine attacked the factions. They were the curse of Italy in mediaeval times, and their ravages are described by the Bollandists in this explicit statement: 'The whole of Italy was torn to pieces by the deadly hatred of ever-recurring factions. There was scarcely a town which did not either fight the neighbouring town, or in which the citizens did not slay each other by the force of party spirit.' The political state of Italy did not offer a natural remedy to so calamitous a state of things, for the Bollandists go on to say, 'To still the bloody hatred which was often carried on by generations, great tact alone did not suffice; the excitement of the citizens needed to be stayed by strong authority, vested in one whose voice had power to assuage divisions.'[159]

It is difficult to see how this need could be met, save by a stable government or the influence of sanctity. John at least gave them the desired treatment. He preached against them with the speaking force of miracles. In 1430 a cruel enmity divided the people of Ortona and Lanciano, and the efforts of the peacemaker seemed to fall powerless upon their hardened hearts. As, according to his custom, he was preaching in the open air before the Church of St. Thomas, he suddenly exclaimed, 'O inhabitants of Ortona, know that as God is to be found there where peace is, so where hatred exists the devil is to be found. And that you may see with your own eyes the truth which I preach to your ears, in the name of Almighty God I call upon that cursed dog to appear.' The result of this solemn interpellation was the appearance of a strange and hideous black dog. No one knew whence he came or whither he vanished, but the Saint attained his end. After the sermon, when he had returned to his monastery, the concourse of penitents would hardly

---

[159] Comment. Praev., p. 284.

allow him to leave the confessional. He established a convent of his reform at Lanciano as a peace-token, calling it by the name of the Holy Angel of Peace.[160] In the same way on another occasion he reconciled the people of Rieti with a neighbouring town. Party spirit had run very high, and many lives had been lost in the quarrel. After the fray, when peace negotiations were pending, a certain man was grievously wounded in the head. The enemy's sword had laid bare his very brain. Medical aid, naturally enough, could do nothing, but John, that 'lover of peace,' approaching the unconscious man, took the wounded head tenderly in his hands and literally put it together whilst he prayed, saying, 'In the name of Jesus Christ, arise, and be sound.'[161]

The barbarity of the times is no doubt an indisputable fact; but comparisons as to the intensity of human wickedness at different epochs are profitless. The evil in those days came to the surface, whereas now it is apt to be ignored beneath a coating of decorum and respectability. Thus such an occurrence as the one we are about to recount almost raises a smile of incredulity by reason of the intensity of the details. Three shepherds in Apulia tempted an unfortunate young man to grievous sin, but he resisting, they put him to death, cooked his flesh, and invited the victim's father, who was in ignorance as to what they had done, to partake of their dish. Towards the end of the meal they disclosed their crime to the unhappy father. It needed the mediation of a saint to make peace between them, and it was not one of John's least

---

[160] *Vita*, p. 456, and *Chronica*, quinta parte, p. 55.
[161] *Vita*, p. 457.

victories to bring it about.[162]

But the regard for legal justice which had formerly distinguished the Governor of Perugia, was now transformed in the Friar into a higher love of truth and righteousness. He was well hated, and there existed those who would willingly have taken his life if God had not preserved it in a miraculous way, and caused his own virtue to shield him from the attacks of evil. It is a sad thought, but one which the history of the saints fully bears out, that no man can love truth for its own sake and not be hated. The Sovereign Pontiff, Martin V, intrusted John with a special mission against the Fraticelli, and in a Bull of the year 1426 made this comment on a sect, which at once recalls the words 'Be not too holy.' 'The Apostolic See,' he says, 'must diligently watch lest the greedy wolf with his thousand artifices should lead the unsuspecting sheep to the pit of perdition.' Further on Martin V alludes to the 'pretext of greater sanctity,' which was so deceptive in the Fraticelli. They had been condemned by John XXII, who saw in that alleged craving for a more rigorous poverty the germ of future Communism. Their system, indeed, was a defection from authority, like all the heretical aberrations of the age. The destruction of all human power would, it is easy to see, strike a heavy blow at the sovereignty of Almighty God over his creatures, and the Fraticelli, who had begun their career by a false aspiration after poverty, ended by teaching that crimes subversive of society were no crimes at all. In the fifteenth century in Italy the sect had assumed the proportions of a heresy, the more pernicious in that

---

[162] Christophorus a Varisio, p. 497.

158

the reputation of the whole Order of the Friars Minor was concerned. John's labours were shared by St. James de Marcia, but the honour of having overcome the Fraticelli belongs chiefly to our Saint, who, viewed as an inquisitor, might almost have said with St. Paul, 'In journeying often, in perils of water, in perils of robbers, in perils from my own nation, in perils from the Gentiles, in perils in the city, in perils in the wilderness, in perils in the sea, in perils from false brethren, in labour and painfulness, in many watchings, in hunger and thirst, in fastings many, in cold and nakedness, besides those things which are without: my daily instance, the solicitude for all the churches.'[163] These false brethren once waylaid him in a solitary place, when he had left his companions in the rear, probably to be able to indulge in prayer. 'Where is John Capistran?' they furiously asked him; and he, frightened at first by their violence, reflected that he would rather die than lie, and answered calmly as our Lord had done in the Garden, 'I am he.' Then fear came upon them too, and they seemed powerless to raise a hand against him. The last survivors of the sect returned to the unity of the Church under Paul II.

It was in 1451 that John responded to the invitation of Frederick III and went to Germany as Papal Legate against the Hussites. This heresy bore a very close resemblance to that of Wycliffe; both were germs of Lutheranism, and the Hussites at least had a political reason of existence. Bohemia was their native place, and the Czech nationality had been seriously wounded by conflicting interests

---

[163] 2 Cor. xi. 26—28.

159

of German, Bavarian, and Saxon claims. John Huss was a Bohemian, born in 1369, and the University of Prague was his intellectual centre and the organ for propagating his opinions. Unfortunately English Wycliffism had produced a greater counter influence there than might have been expected in those days of laborious communication, by the marriage of Richard II with Anne of Bohemia in 1381. That authority is dependent on virtue was the chief thesis of Wycliffe's teaching, and the Hussites took an erroneous notion of predestination as their standing-point, and talked in vague language of the mystical Church of the Elect. They were also known as Bohemians from their origin and country, and whilst they gave a body to the spirit of independence which was afloat, they were not only heretics, but enemies of order, and politically dangerous. So the Apostle of Peace was summoned by Frederick III to use the same arms which had already proved victorious in Italy over the Fraticelli, the greatest of these being charity. In striking contrast to the populations which welcomed him with ovations on the road to Vienna, and greeted him with the words, *'Benedictus qui venit in nomine Domini,'* were the persecutions he endured for loving justice and hating iniquity. He worked many conversions in Moravia and Silesia, showing forth the power of the truth by his sanctity and his miracles. Nicolas V sent him unlimited faculties, which only enraged the Bohemians the more. They revenged themselves by painting caricatures of John, 'sometimes with women, sometimes with devils,'[164] and by denouncing him as 'a seducer, Antichrist, a devil incarnate.' When the report of

---

[164] Christophorus a Varisio, p. 501.

these things reached the Saint he smiled, and, lifting up his hands, prayed to God to spare his enemies. John, however, never succeeded in reaching Prague, the hotbed of the heresy. When in his zeal he begged for admittance there, 'We would rather welcome a hundred thousand devils,' was the civil answer. 'Since I may not go to Prague,' replied the Apostle, 'in a short time my little dogs shall find access there.' He alluded prophetically to his disciples and those whom he had received into the Order, who in point of fact did succeed later in founding a monastery at Prague.[165]

Shaking off the dust of Bohemia, he turned to Hungary, which was then a prey to the Photian Schism. There, in the midst of a spiritual work of mercy, he was overtaken by the aggressive Turk, and proved a hero as well as an apostle.

To the numberless fatigues of his life, as we have attempted to describe it, with the anxious welfare of souls upon his heart from morning till evening, the Holy See added other toils. Four times John was called upon to exercise special missions requiring great prudence and delicacy. The Order of the Jesuati had been established in 1364, but in Pope Eugenius IV's time it lay under the ban of grievous charges. St. John Capistran and St. Lawrence Justinian were deputed to Venice to examine the accusations with all possible care, and they decided justly that these were not grounded. Two centuries later, in 1668, the Order was finally suppressed by Clement IX.

---

[165] Christophorus a Varisio, p. 501.

There were tears in the chalice of Eugenius IV. The Congress at Bâle had enacted the farce of electing another Antipope. The great schism had left a remnant of mischief, like a nervous affection after the real malady has been cured. The candidate chosen by Bâle, which, as an assembly, courted favour and lacked money, was Amadeus, Duke of Savoy, a layman not sufficiently gifted with humour to refuse the position. He called himself Felix V. John's mission was to the powerful Duke of Milan, Filippo Maria Sforza, and to Philip, Duke of Burgundy, who, Eugenius had reasons for fearing, would espouse the cause of Amadeus. But in this particular instance his suspicions appear to have been ungrounded. Filippo Maria was blessed with the usual sagacity of the Sforzas, and John's mission consisted in strengthening the adhesion of the two dukes, who werenearly connected by marriage to Eugenius.

In the early part of 1444, John was deputed to Sicily on another matter connected with the election of Bâle. Alphonsus, King of Aragon, had been adopted by Joanna II as her heir, and he wished in this capacity to obtain the Papal Investiture against the candidate of the Holy See, Réné of Anjou. Eugenius resisted till the threatening attitude of Alphonsus, and his overtures to Amadeus, induced him to sacrifice his inclination to the good of the Church.

Throughout the middle ages the ecclesiastical statutes against the Jews were very severe. Perhaps in no other department has the famous adage of St. Augustine, 'Hate the error, love the man,' received a better exemplification than in

162

the Holy See's conduct towards the once chosen people. Whilst guarding all Christians against that melancholy perversity, and forbidding to a certain extent social intercourse between the two,[166] the question of harming the Jews never arose but the Sovereign Pontiff immediately stepped forward as the champion of their persons. Now, however, Nicholas V, successor to Eugenius IV, had an eye to the spiritual good of Christians in enforcing certain laws established by the Holy See relating to the 'error.' 'Whereas,' his Bull ran, 'it is a small thing to make laws unless their execution be committed to sure hands, We depute, institute, and ordain Our beloved son, Friar John of Capistran, of the Friars Minor, to be charged with the supervision of all former decrees in virtue of Our Apostolic authority.'[167] The date of this mandate was 1447, and one fact amongst others proves that the Holy Father's confidence was merited. In 1450, being about to leave Rome, John was challenged by a learned rabbi to an argument. When the appointed time arrived, Gamaliel, this was his name, appeared not alone, but with forty companions. He distorted certain texts of the Old Testament, and thought he was going to achieve an easy victory over John's religion. Instead of this issue, the Saint converted Gamaliel and his forty co-religionists into soldiers of Jesus Christ.

Two little anecdotes give the character of

---

[166] 'Nempe prohibebantur Judaei blasphemare nomen Christi, ejus Genitricis et aliorum Sanctorum, usuras a Christianis exigere: vicissim Christianis interdictum erat, a Judaeis medicinas recipere, communibus uti balneis cum iisdem, et his similia.')*Comment. Praev. in vitam*, p. 291).
[167] Comment, p. 291.

this apostolical man better than many words. Once, in Moravia, it chanced that he passed by a place where five men had recently been executed. Their bodies were still hanging up, and as he begged that they might be taken down and given decent burial, a sudden horror fell upon him at the terrible sight of that poor mortality which bore the marks of a violent death. He quickly stifled the first movement of nature by clasping those bodies already fetid to his heart. Instead of the odour of death, he drew a sweet fragrance from that embrace, which charity had prompted. Here was one side of his character. On another occasion he was walking through a cemetery in the province of Abbruzzo, and it happened that a woman of bad character had been buried there, an act which was contrary to the practice of those times. The Saint was informed of the fact, and immediately declared that her body must be taken up out of consecrated ground. The saying seemed a hard one to some, and John was obliged to prove his opinion with his eloquence. He rarely spoke in vain. The woman's remains were removed, and thrown into a field, 'like those of a beast.'[168]

Few love justice in our times, because few hate iniquity, for the love and the hatred are correlative, not existing apart. Long ago the Psalmist declared that justice and peace had embraced, which in his typical language signified that a time would come when the letter of his prophecy should be carried out in the life of God's saints.

---

[168] Christophorus a Varisio, p. 515.

CHAPTER XII.

Looking through the Microscope.

The saints see the spiritual creation through a microscope. The world of nature all around is in the richness of its details no more discoverable to the naked eye than the vegetation, if we may so speak, with which God surrounds and encloses souls. In proportion as a microscope is powerful are its capabilities of making visible what would otherwise be hidden, and by the very force of things it cannot represent a lie. What seemed to be the purest water will be seen to be the full of the minutest animalculae, and the tiniest thing visible will attain in this process almost respectable proportions. The special achievement of the microscope is to represent to us things in nature whose existence we did not surmise. In the spiritual life from the very beginning there have been some chosen servants of God who also have seen things unseen by the many, but nevertheless as they really exist in the world of souls. Simplicity and purity, those two eyes of the higher nature, are the focus through which they look at men, angels, and devils, two orders of beings of whom the better among us possess only a half consciousness, while the worse see them not at all. Many times in reading of the wonderful insight vouchsafed to John Capistran it will be necessary to bear in mind that he belonged to the race of gazers through the microscope. The glass of fresh water suddenly discovered to be full of life is to the savage as little explicable as the most wonderful and intuitive vision of the saints is to the sinner. Neither can be explained, but we may well argue by analogy from the physical creation.

Wonderful as it is, its existence cannot be questioned, neither can the hidden spiritual creation be doubted, surpassing though it does the physical in the same degree as the soul is of a higher order than the body. Are we not 'better than many sparrows?'

According to St. Augustine a threefold power is given to the apostle: viz., over nature to cure it, over devils to thrust them out, over the elements to change them. John was always a lavish wonderworker, and there was with him a profusion of supernatural graces for others, extraordinary even in the annals of the saints. Almighty God seemed after a certain manner to proportion the temporal cures of His servant to that spiritual renovation which he carried out on so large a scale. But is it not always thus? The power of curing those who are sick rests on one of a higher order, that of giving health to diseased souls. Hence, however numerous visible miracles might be, the invisible ones would always preponderate.

Like St. Bernardine, John induced men to renounce 'dice and other games of the kind, and he preached a return to former modesty in correcting the excessive style of dress, both of men and women, especially their head-gear.' And again the same biographer, who was an eye-witness of what he relates, says, 'I once saw at Nuremberg six large coaches full of gambling tables being taken to the common marketplace, where there were also more than seventy painted carriages, which were employed in the winter for wicked purposes, causing many crimes. These were all consumed by fire in the presence of all the people.'[169] The Saint brought about similar results generally in the large towns with the same vigorous spirit. No half measures satisfied him. He gave no quarter to the instruments of gambling and articles of vanity and superfluous finery. It is to be feared that when the system of total abstinence is acted upon in the reformation of manners, it indicates no small amount of depravity.

If John's apostolic authority worked so great a change in Catholics, his influence over incipient Protestantism was no less striking. Four thousand Hussite priests abjured their heresy at his feet,[170] whilst he reaped a harvest of sixteen thousand of their number to the Church.

These were the miracles of his right hand; now let us see what, following out the comparison, might be called those of his left, and how far his outward life bore the three marks of the Apostle.

As he was preaching once in a field on the confines of Lombardy, the air and atmosphere announced the coming of a storm. His audience showed signs of restlessness, but John bade them be still, for he had prayed to God not to allow the rain to interfere with his sermon. The storm fell like a deluge upon the surrounding country, but not a drop of rain was felt within the arena of his listeners. In place of the tears of nature it was the tears of sinners, and many followed him in consequence of the prodigy. The clean of heart alone may claim obedience from God's elements. One day the devil,

---

[169] Nicolaus de Fara.

[170] St. John's letter to the University of Vienna.

says the chronicle, stirred up the crickets and swallows to drown the preacher's words, but he reckoned without his master. John, like his holy Father Francis, calmly imposed silence on the animals, and they obeyed him well enough to deserve his blessing at the end of the sermon. These discourses in the open air were naturally subject to many outward impediments. On another occasion a furious bull tossed a poor woman and left her in a state which was past natural remedies. But John, taking her by the hand, exhorted her to arise, and brought her back to life. Let not the comparison of the microscope be forgotten. John's spiritual vision could see the heinousness of vice, as we by our faith know that it exists, and at times God permitted him to draw the veil between faith and its reality from before the eyes of sinners; in other words, to clothe crime in a sensible form. At Aquila, for instance, the devils appeared in visible shape at the command of the wonder-worker, and a most extraordinary story is told of the deliverance of a certain woman from possession. John was preaching during a Lent against the vanity in dress, which had there assumed the proportions of a soul-destroying passion, and one day this woman was brought to him to be cured of the cruel slavery. He commanded her in the spirit of faith to thrust out 'the servant who had possession of her house.' She vomited a loathsome worm, in which the Saint, looking through the microscope, recognized the demon of vanity, who had worked terrible ravages at Aquila. Another woman in the same state was brought to him in Venice. She hurled rather than shrieked these words at him: 'Woe to me to-day through thee, Capistran.' The saint freed her from the service of the Evil One in the name of Jesus.[171]

The miraculous cures wrought by John were numbered by hundreds, and no better notion can be given of them than by citing the action of one of his companions, who, after noting down seven hundred, threw away his pen in despair. Among the first probably was one which he worked three years after his entrance into religion on a poor madman whom he chanced to encounter in the cloisters of his convent. He blessed the man and restored him to health. A poor paralytic who could not make a single movement was taken to the church where the Saint was to pass. John quickly found him out, saying,

'What is the matter, you poor man?' And he explaining his state, commended himself to the servant of God.

'If it were the Divine will that you should remain in this state, would you agree?'

'Surely I would, Father.'

'What grace do you desire?' again asked the Saint.

' That I may be able to get as far as the church and the doctor's.'

'Have confidence in God,' answered the Saint, 'you shall obtain a far greater grace,' and

---

[171] Nicolaus de Fara, p. 452.

taking him by the hand he restored him so completely to strength that the man said he was prepared to run two miles.[172]

When in 1451 John left Italy for ever, he proceeded through Carinthia and Styria to Vienna, where he preached on the feast of Corpus Christi to a multitude of one hundred thousand, according to his historian. There seems, however, to have been some exaggeration or a want of accurateness in his biographers every time they tried to fix the number of his hearers. He was at Vienna when a certain little girl of three years old, after straying from her parents, was found quite dead in a well. The mother's words on looking upon her child were full of faith, and they prove the fame of St. John at a time when communication was so difficult. 'I have heard,' she said to her brother, 'that a holy man, an Italian, has lately come to Vienna, by whom Almighty God works numerous miracles. I pray of you let us take him this dead child, for I hope he will restore her to us alive.' The little girl was presented to the Saint on the altar steps after Mass amongst the other sick whom John then touched and blessed, merely for devotion's sake, as his official cures, if the phrase may be used, did not take place till after the sermon. When, however, the mother uncovered the little body she found that her child breathed again. She cried aloud in her joy, but others cried too, and there was a bustle amongst the congregation who were falling into their places for the sermon. Nicolas de Fara himself saw the child who owed her life to so great a miracle, and although she was a peasant by birth, he asserts that she looked more 'like a

---

[172] *Vita*, p. 458.

prince's daughter,'[173] and when he questioned her mother as to her appearance, he was told that her beauty had risen with her from the dead, and that previously she had not been a pretty child. In the same year an immense crowd gathered round the Saint on the Day of Pentecost. The feast seemed to warrant great expectations, and the usual petitioners did not fail to profit by the solemnity of the day. But it passed by without a single cure, and in the evening the holy Father, reviewing his day, used these remarkable words, which bear a resemblance to those of our Lord, 'The power has gone out of me,' he said, 'I am quite tired out, and to-day nothing has been done.' One of his disciples, mistaking this for discouragement, quickly answered, 'Do not be astonished, Father, perhaps God wished to try your patience.' Some, indeed, of his companions openly expressed their disappointment that so great a feast had been so bare of visible results, but they were silenced by John. 'O ye of little faith! why do you doubt? Tomorrow you shall see the glory and the magnificence of the great God.' The next day, as he had foretold, twenty men went forth cured from his touch. 'We saw them with our eyes and felt them with our hands,' remarks the same biographer.[174]

Of all German towns Wratislau, the capital of Silesia, was most devoted to our Saint, who reciprocated the affection. But Wratislau had its Hussite faction, and one day these heretics, together with certain false Catholics, bethought themselves of playing John a trick. They brought him a living man

---

[173] 'Quasi principis filia videretur.' (p. 458).
[174] Nicolaus de Fara, p. 331.

on a bier in the midst of funeral pomp, and pretended to sue for his resurrection. The Saint, who was not deceived, replied, 'Let him remain with the dead for all eternity.' 'See,' exclaimed at once the Hussites, 'the sanctity of this man, who cannot raise the dead to life. Now you shall discover that we have got still holier men amongst our party.' But when they were called, and had commanded Peter, such was the name of the pretender, to arise from the bier, his spirit had really departed.

Scoffers at his miraculous powers met with evident punishment from Heaven. A certain man, who would not believe what he might have seen for himself, one day said in jest, 'I will believe these miracles which I hear about when my blind dog gets back his sight.' No sooner had he spoken than the dog recovered his eyesight, but he became suddenly blind. Instances of sudden death are recorded in consequence of the same incredulous spirit. The only lawful objection which a reasonable Catholic may make on first hearing of a miraculous occurrence, is to say, for instance, ' I know it might happen, but whether it did is another question.' Incredulity, on the contrary, tries hard to prove that such things are simply impossible.

In the saints prophetical knowledge of events is so often allied with miraculous power that it can be no matter of astonishment to find that a wonderworker of St. John's stature was also a prophet. When Martin V lay dangerously ill the Saint went to visit him, and on leaving the room he saw a shining light, where the words, 'he shall not behold the coming dawn ' were written. Before the elevation of Eugenius IV to the Holy See John said to him one day in a familiar conversation, 'I shall not see you again except as Sovereign Pontiff.' And one year before the end of Eugenius' Pontificate, John, who had few things more at heart than the canonization of Bernardine, announced the realization of his wish to the same Pope, 'Another shall come after you, most Holy Father, who will canonize blessed Bernardine.' [175] He alluded to Nicholas V, whose election he also foretold.

In the convent of *Ara Coeli* there was a friar in great renown for extraordinary graces and holy life, and Eugenius, then Sovereign Pontiff, expressed a wish to see him. Admitted to a long audience, Friar Justin was treated with a loving familiarity by the Head of the Church, and dismissed at length with a present of relics; but the friar's virtue was not built upon the rock of humility. He began to fancy that he was too good for the intercourse of his brethren, and returned to the convent, his heart full of pride. On the way he happened to meet John, who, by his supernatural intuition, saw what was going on. 'Alas, alas, Brother Justin,' he exclaimed, 'you entered the Apostolic Palace an angel, and you come out a demon. May God have mercy on you.'[176] The friar was very irate at the reproof, but his subsequent career justified the Saint's warning. His fall was the greater in proportion to his vocation, for a bad religious presents the worse type of a sinner. God tried him with the favour of the great, and found him wanting. He expiated his crimes by dying in a prison.

---

[175] Nicolaus de Fara, p. 460.
[176] Chronica, p. 49.

To the credulous race of philosophers[177] too numerous in our days, and to men whose minds are rather open to mathematics than to history, some of the anecdotes recorded in this chapter might appear in the light of fables, the vagaries of its religious imagination preserved by a believing age. Supposing, indeed, the authenticity of St. John's authority over devils could by some impossibility be called in question, what then? The legends which meet us in the lives of the Saints represent the general belief of the ages to which the Saints belong, and that general belief represents a Providential law, which is not dependent for its proof upon this or that particular instance in which it may be thought to be exemplified. The true objection of the writers of whom we speak is to the law, and not to the instances of its working. We fear that the world in general echoes Cicero's words, 'Confess anything rather than that there is a Divine Providence.'[178]

CHAPTER XIII.

The Turk in 1455.

In attempting in the last chapter to describe rather the manner than the order of John's apostolate, we must now take up chronologically the thread of his life, and see what were the great and all-absorbing interests of his latter years.

---

[177] 'Philosophorum credula gens.'

[178] 'Quidvis denique potius, quam Deos res humanas curare fateamur' (De Divinatione, 1. i. c. xvii.).

'The zeal of Thy House hath consumed me' might fitly be applied to John Capistran. From his thirty-first to his seventy-first year the one thing which presented anything like the appearance of a human longing was his ardour in the cause of St. Bernardine's canonization; but God's honour and glory purified even this craving of his heart. For the space of six years after Bernardine's holy death in 1444, John worked unceasingly that the voice of the Church might put its seal upon his sanctity. He identified himself to so great an extent with his friend, that, in the inquiry into the miracles, some wrought by John were attributed to Bernardine, and, as we have said elsewhere, he sheltered his own miraculous power under the wing of what he considered superior holiness. The difficulties and heart-burnings peculiar to a labour of this kind hardly had any weight in the ardent mind of Friar John; a thing which he desired, and which related to God's glory, was as good as half done, and when the friars would have laid down their arms in discouragement, John never lost confidence. He had a habit of saying quaintly, 'Blessed Bernardine, pray for thyself.'[179] The process was carried on during the Pontificates of Eugenius IV and Nicholas V, John putting his hand vigorously to the work by his negotiations with cardinals, bishops, and others. On one occasion he said to Nicholas V, 'Take Blessed Bernardine's body and me with it, and cast us into the fire. If we are burnt, put it down to my sins, but if we are preserved, interpret it as an expression of God's will.' Nicholas V, different in character from our apostle, was as much a passive advocate for

---

[179] 'Beate Bernardine, ora pro te' (Vita, Auctore Christophoro a Varisio).

peace as John was an active instrument in the same cause. His words to his friends after his election had been, 'I pray that God may give me grace to accomplish the wish of my heart, that is, to use no other arms during my Pontificate but the Cross of Jesus Christ.'[180] The Pontiff and his assistants were much moved by the Saint's words, but John had another enemy to contend with whose negative support he considered almost as important to secure for Bernardine as the Holy See. A certain lay-brother of the Observance, Brother Thomas of Florence, had lately died in the odour of sanctity, and now many sick persons, who could not get to Aquila, satisfied themselves by obtaining their cure of the same Brother Thomas at Rieti. John fairly took fright at these wonders, for he not unreasonably argued, 'It will be said at Rome, "All the Friars of the Observance want to work miracles," and consequently those of Bernardine would stand a poorer chance of consideration. So he betook himself to the tomb of the wonder-working lay-brother at Rieti, and in his simplicity besought him to be so good as to leave off endangering Bernardine's cause.' 'Blessed Thomas,' he said, 'in life you were always obedient, and never went against the wishes of your superiors. In virtue, therefore, of holy obedience I command you to abstain from any more miracles, because they might hinder Blessed Bernardine's canonization.' Almighty God heard this strange prayer, for it was remarked that the lay-brother gave way entirely to St. Bernardine, and worked no more miracles.[181]

---

[180] Christophe, *Histoire de la Papauté pendant le XVième Siécle.*, t. i. p. 372.
[181] Christophorus a Varisio, p. 510.

Whilst John was so busily engaged, he had a vision in which the object of all this devotion Bernardine himself appeared. A friar happened to disturb the colloquy by coming into John's cell at the time: 'May God spare you, Brother,' he exclaimed, 'I was talking to the Blessed Bernardine.' One day Nicholas V could not resist saying to this zealous friend, 'Who will labour for your own canonization, Father John? ' 'I am a sinner,' he answered, 'and to such these honours are not due.' But the bishops deputed for the cause thought otherwise. Considering John's purity and holiness, they judged him to be almost ripe for canonization himself. [182] In 1450, before John set out for Germany, he had the happiness of seeing the fulfilment of this dream of his heart. Nicholas V solemnly placed Bernardine of Siena on the catalogue of the saints.

Another labour less characteristic of the man, but quite as significant of the saint, was the reform of the Observance, because it condenses into a comparatively small sphere the true notion of reformation. Whilst innovators were defying the principle of authority, and thus striking a blow at all the institutions which belong to the growth of the spiritual power, a saint grasped at one notion as if it had been a plank to save his Order from the waters of that heretical outpour. John's zeal for the Observance meant this. There is one virtue which represents flavour-giving salt to the Church. It is that of holy chastity, which in its perfection implies humility and charity in their highest degree. 'If the salt lose its flavour, wherewith shall the earth be

---

[182] Christophorus a Varisio, p. 511

177

salted?' History seems to authorize the statement that every heresy has been influenced, if not brought about, by its neglect, and it can therefore be no wonder that a Catholic reformer should have laboured so energetically to raise the standard of the spiritual life. On the expiration of Bernardine's Vicariate in 1441, John was appointed his successor as Vicar-General of the Observance, and these two Saints between them attained their object, one comparatively small, it may be, in our eyes, but great in itself. Through their efforts a body of men appeared working in the world, though not of it, whose life was in contradiction to the actual spirit of pride and luxury, who in the midst of moral corruption showed forth the fruits of that Catholic teaching against the restraints of which the pre-reformers were already murmuring. John sometimes confided to Pope Eugenius his distress and grief at the relaxation and division of his order, and when the Holy Father inquiringly asked how he proposed to reform it, the Saint answered, 'With the abolition of three P's.'[183] This enigmatical reply puzzled Eugenius, and John further explained his meaning. 'By the first P, Holy Father, I mean profligacy; by the second, petulancy; by the third, purse: the three spirits of impurity, disobedience, and simony.' If John could have fully carried out this programme, and extended it to all Orders in the Church, we venture to say there would have been nothing left for Luther to destroy. He founded several provinces of the Observance, and many convents in Germany and Poland, and truly his 'little dogs' (catuli), that is, his brethren and disciples in religion, in one case at least, effected what he himself would have carried

---

[183] 'Pueros, petulantiam, pecuniam.'

out, by making their way into Prague. One of the Saint's last thoughts in this world was for his dear Observance. He left it a triple recommendation as a legacy : 'Let them keep a zeal for religion, the fervour of charity, and strict discipline.'[184]

It is self-evident that under any circumstances peace must be a blessing; but when John went to Germany in 1451, at the invitation of the Emperor Frederick III, there had perhaps never been a time when it was of higher political importance to restore unity amongst European princes. The Roman Empire of the West had been dead a thousand years, and if that of the East had enjoyed a longer existence, and was still, so to say, breathing, if not living, it was owing to the splendid position of Constantinople. Sancta Sophia was undermined by heresy and schism, and when Mahomet II, a ferocious son of the Prophet, came with the match, the work of destruction quickly followed. In 1453, the last Christian sovereign of Constantinople, Constantine Paleologus, better than his race as he happened to be, fell in the ruin of his family; and the Ottoman Turks obtained that firm footing in Europe which they have ever since retained. Divine Providence had willed that they should rise to something like pre-eminence just at the very time when the authority of the Holy See became weakened, and in the middle of the fifteenth century Europe was so engrossed by national dissensions as to pay a very deaf ear to the Pontiffs, who alone seemed to realize the gravity of the situation. Something may be said to exonerate the Christian Powers. It is this. The Greeks, like the boy

---

[184] Comment, p. 399.

in the fable, had cried 'wolf' so often that false alarms had weakened their cause. They were a fickle and perfidious race, vain of their effete civilization and literary pre-eminence, scorning the Latins as half-bred barbarians, using them in time of need to fight their battles, and making profit of them wherever this was possible. The Crusades had given indeed a not very flattering measure of their capabilities. They invited the Latins to help them, and then threw obstacles in the way of progress, so that perhaps in no other instance should we be so tempted to exclaim that the God of Catholics and the God of heretics are not identical. In the very first Crusade the Emperor of Constantinople made a secret alliance with the Turks and Saracens against the Latins, for the conduct of the Greeks said, 'Better is the Crescent than the Pope of Rome.' The danger over, they returned to their ill-defined policy, held on to their schism by the force of religious hatred and national sympathy, to fall at last as they would probably never have done had they not earned the contempt of Europe by their weakness, and held off the Latins by their exclusiveness. It is true the Latins had made an attempt at retaliation by taking Constantinople after the fourth Crusade in the thirteenth century; but their acts of violence had been quite against the spirit of the Sovereign Pontiff, who had published a written protest disclaiming the work of his adherents. Whereas the undercurrent of popular sympathy at Constantinople was rather with the Turk than with the Successor of Peter, the Popes had always been the avowed enemy of the Crescent. When they could do nothing else they protested against that religious power which was the more to be dreaded by reason of its very earnestness. In

1394 Boniface IX published a Bull in which he bewailed the sins of Christendom as having drawn down a punishment from Heaven in the shape of ever-recurring attacks from the Ottomans. 'The mind,' he says, 'is horrified at the very mention of these miseries, but it crowns our anguish to reflect that the whole of Christendom, which, if in concord, might put an end to these and even greater evils, is either in open war, country with country, or, if in apparent peace, is secretly wasted by mutual jealousies and animosities.'[185] Precisely the same evils, with regard to the Turks, were signalized by Eugenius IV in 1442. The Ottomans had conquered Thrace, Macedonia, Epirus, Albania, and Bulgaria, they threatened Europe, and we might almost fancy we were reading a newspaper account of Bulgarian atrocities in that Encyclical Letter of more than four hundred years ago. Moses, then, who was watching the fight from the mountain, gave frequent and earnest warning; but Christendom— for it existed then — was occupied with enemies at home. England had been fighting useless battles with France, ornamenting herself with tawdry finery, but after the inglorious pile at Rouen, her renown, such as it was, began to wane. The days of Crecy and Poitiers and Agincourt were followed by the calamitous Wars of the Roses. France was engaged in winning back her territory from English usurpers during a long period of strife, called in her history the hundred years' war. Spain could hardly hold up her head against the Saracens, but used all her energy over and above to win the Kingdom of Naples. The Hussites in Germany formed a discordant element, powerful enough to

---

[185] The Very Rev. Dr. Newman, *The Turks*, p. 177.

put into requisition all home energies; and with shame it must be said, that the only response in the west of Europe to the Holy Father's cry of alarm was that of certain Italian cities, who feared for their possessions in the Levant. Of these, Pisa, Genoa, and Venice were the foremost. Germany held Diets and voted subsidies, which never appeared, for the new crusaders. Hungary was more generous. Wladislaus, King of Poland, had been called to the Hungarian crown through the exertions of John Corvin Hunyad, who became his right hand in political as well as military emergencies. No one could dispute Huniady's capacity on the field of battle, but in the council-chamber he possessed less sharp -sightedness, and whilst the King and his Minister made Hungary glorious in its well-nigh single-handed efforts against the Ottomans, they committed the fault too of first signing an inopportune peace at Szegedin, and then of breaking it without a cause, thus falling into the snare of giving the Turks, under the formidable Amurath, a certain ground for complaint. After two almost splendid victories against the common enemy in 1443, Wladislaus and Huniady listened to the too egotistical representations of a Servian prince, George Brankowitz, who had been banished from his domains by Amurath. He made zeal against the Turk a cover for personal interests, and brought about a ten years' treaty of peace signed at Szegedin, by which the Sultan Amurath, who detected his foible, restored him to his possessions in Servia on condition that he should negotiate for the Turks. Never was peace more fatal to Christian interests. Instead of allowing Hungary to pursue her advantages, it on the contrary gave the Turks just the breathing-time they needed to recruit their forces. As the Servian Prince had been the means of this untimely peace, so another personage, with very different views, urged that it should not be kept. This was the Pope's Legate, Cardinal Caesarini, whose eloquence gave strength to arguments necessarily weak in the presence of the royal oath to keep the armistice. Varna was the consequence of the unwise policy: Caesarini and Wladislaus perished in the fight, and the walls of Constantinople received the first shock of the coming disaster in 1453.

To Eugenius IV succeeded in 1447 Nicholas V, a Pontiff whose watchword was peace. Various negotiators were despatched to allay the grand obstacle to the Turks, want of unity amongst Christians. In this state of things Cardinal Isidore appeared in Constantinople in its last Christian days in 1453, to urge the acceptance of terms of union; but the Greeks made the Emperor's position a thorny one. Divided between threatening dangers, the heretical sympathies of his people, and his personal wish to satisfy the Pope, he almost necessarily rendered unavailing the last attempt to save the Greeks. Thus the sentiments of the people of Constantinople expressed by the aphorism: 'Better the Crescent than the Tiara,' was confirmed by an imperial Amen, forced by circumstances upon Paleologus.

Cardinal Capranica was charged with the reconciliation of the Genoese and the King of Aragon. Nicholas tried to pacify the King of Portugal by the present of the Golden Rose, and despatched Cardinal d'Estouteville to France to mediate with the French King, and lastly our St.

John Capistran had a double mission in Germany, in bringing about political and religious peace. The sixteen thousand Hussites, whom he converted from their heresy, surely had something to say to the future victory at Belgrade.

But now the succession in Hungary was again unsettled by the premature death of Wladislaus. The heir to the throne, Ladislaus, son of Albech II., had lived from his infancy at the Court of Frederick III, who evidently meant to keep him there, with probable views of his own upon the youthful prince's kingdom. In vain the Hungarians and Bohemians asked for the return of their King. Frederick's obstinate refusal occasioned a very comprehensible ill-will, an attitude of hostility between the two nations which formed a barrier against unity. Their pacification was the work of Nicholas V, and under him, of John Capistran and the Papal Legate. Then in 1455, Callistus III succeeded to the Apostolic See at a time ominous enough to have shaken the courage of the bravest, for although Nicholas had paved the way to universal pacification, the great enemy was still there, the Ottoman Turks, and they only awaited a favourable opportunity for pursuing the advantage gained by them at Varna. Callistus III was that very Pope to whom St. Vincent Ferrer had predicted his elevation long years before. He rang out through the whole world of Christianity the alarm bell or the Turk's bell, as it was originally called, and which ever since has become a part of the daily life of Catholics. The *Angelus* was instituted to the sound of war, just as the feast of the Rosary was founded to commemorate the struggle. Even in our most peaceful devotions here on earth we pray within hearing of the battlefield; *bella premunt hostilia* finds its place in the deep calmness of the *O Salutaris*. Callistus made personal efforts for the Crusade in equipping a fleet at the expense of the Holy See, and in causing the sacred vessels of the principal churches in Rome to be melted down for the purpose of ready money. He had expected great things of the French King, Charles VII, but the sovereigns of the time were plunged in a strange apathy. They were losing the generous spirit of enterprise which distinguished the middle ages, and had induced monarchs to sacrifice their ease and comfort to the Holy Sepulchre. So it came to pass that whereas the Crusades had placed a motive of faith before men to spur them on to their best efforts, now that it was a question of personal danger the great ones of Europe mostly slumbered and slept.

There are tears in our Saint's letter to Callistus, dated from a town in Austria, on this indifference, for he says: 'In these parts no man troubles himself on the subject. The Bishop of Pavia has laboured, and the Bishop of Siena has toiled, not to speak of what I have done. Poland, Bohemia, Moravia, Austria, Bavaria were represented first at the Diet of Ratisbon, then at Frankfort, at Vienna, then at the Diet of Neustadt[186] in presence of the august Emperor (Frederick III). Finally it was determined that nothing can be done this year, but next year about the Ascension they say they will make preparations. . . . O most Holy Father, have pity on the tears and sighs of the Greeks and the Russians, who are taken and sold like brute animals,

---

[186] An outskirt of Vienna.

perhaps by a judgment of God on account of their errors and their schism; have pity on the weak sex, virgins, married women, widows, or orphans as the case may be; have pity on Italy and all Christian people; remove all obstacles, lest a similar lot fall upon us through tardy measures, like a tempest leading to destruction. Would that I, useless and miserable creature, could serve, I will not say as a shield or a breast-plate, but as a bit of dirt beneath the horses' hoofs of those who fight for Christ. I have often been asked by the King, and princes both temporal and spiritual, to go to Hungary; the Emperor, Papal Legates, the Governor of Hungary, John Hunyad, and the other barons have seconded the invitation. Wherefore, unless the Holy and Apostolic See should require otherwise, I have promised to go, and am even now on the way, proposing to reach Buda before the feast of Pentecost (which fell that year on the 25th of May). I, a most miserable creature, prostrate myself at the feet of your Holiness, that you may dispose of my poor services unto life or death. From the town of Judenburg, in the province of Austria, on the feast of the Apostles SS. Philip and James, May 1st, 1455.'[187]

Two things are remarkable in this letter. The Saint appeals to the Holy Father as if he could dispel all difficulties, and speaks of himself as if he were entirely useless. It is a kind of illustration of the manner in which the saints are accustomed to act, praying as if they could do nothing, and labouring as if they could move mountains. John is silent in his letter about the supernatural intimation he had

---

[187] Comment. Praev. p. 357.

received to go to Hungary. After one of those disappointing Diets, that of Frankfort, which as usual, had used big words and been exceedingly empty in results, something approaching to discouragement seems to have entered the Saint's heart. He was uncertain whither he should turn his steps for the greater good of souls, and in this state he fell asleep. Then under the form of a dream he had a vision of his end. He saw that his death was to be caused, not by the actual shedding of blood, but by a martyrdom of desire. The next morning at Mass and during his sermon he heard mysterious voices, which said: 'To Hungary, to Hungary!' There, according to his letter, he arrived towards the end of May, 1455, and 'was received with apostolical honours to the sound of bells, in the midst of flowers and lighted candles. John, that Mover of humility,' sought to escape these ovations by innocent artifices, and where they did not answer, we find St. Vincent's motto on his lips: *Non nobis, Domine, non nobis, sed nomini tuo da gloriam.* The reception given to John seemed a kind of gratitude by anticipation; he came indeed by Divine inspiration in order to save Hungary, his spiritual arms being seconded by the presence of a hero in the person of John Hunyad. One was the sword, the other the heart of the expedition, and both were equally necessary to each other. In the disputed succession, Hunyad had been a loyal partisan of the youthful King, and when Ladislaus died without issue, a son of Hunyad ascended the throne of Hungary. He was at once warrior and Prime Minister with the privileges of a *maire du palais*, a position only possible there where the principle of hereditary royalty has not been firmly established. Without John Hunyad's invincible courage, even the fiery exhortations of John Capistran must have been empty of results, and without the moral victory with which John Capistran began the material fight, probably John Hunyad would have vainly sought to appease the God of armies. St. John laboured for the Crusade by the light of eternal things, and therefore he did not rest content with merely distributing the Cross, which duly arrived from Pope Callistus early in the year 1456, to as many as he could possibly find to take it. The grand secret of all victory he knew to be moral renovation, and he carried on his work of conversion in the very teeth of the Turk. His converts from schism in Hungary are counted by thousands. Later, in the Christian camp, where John's holy influence had done its work, a remarkable decorum and piety reigned amongst the Crusaders. Licentiousness was banished, and even works of supererogation were practised to the constant and ardent war-cry of the apostle, the Holy Name of Jesus.[188] It was this purity of life which lent vigour to the small band of Christians who were to face the ferocious Mahomet II in the glory of his army of one hundred and fifty thousand fanatical Turks. Their number cannot be accurately estimated, but the Poles numbered five hundred men, whilst the Hungarians, who followed John, formed a somewhat undisciplined multitude. The flower of the army, probably the regular troops, were the followers of Hunyad. According to some accounts the whole is reckoned at sixty thousand men.

Since the taking of Constantinople the ambition of Mahomet II knew no bounds. 'There is

---

[188] *Account of Joannes Tagliacotus*, p. 373.

one God in Heaven, there must be one master on earth,' was the terrible threat, which, counting upon easy victory, he openly proclaimed. He had sworn by the Prophet that in two months time he would hold a banquet at Buda. Belgrade, situated on the conflux of two rivers, the Danube and the Save, was the door to Hungary, and already the Turks had advanced up the Danube as far as this important post. They had brought all kind of instruments of war to bear upon the rough and poorly-armed Crusaders. Two terrible machines, twenty-eight feet in length, are mentioned, and seven others, which poured forth a volley of stones day and night. The siege of Belgrade lasted forty days. Its fortifications were levelled to the ground, and a trembling despair had entered into the hearts of the Christians. On the eve of the battle, Hunyad himself came late at night to the Saint saying that his last resources had been tried and had failed. 'I have done everything I could. Now I am breaking down, nor is any means of defence left to us . . . the fortifications are all destroyed, the door lies open to the Turks. We are few compared to so great a multitude, and our men are inexperienced, weak, poor, and timid: the leaders do not agree, what is to be done?' John replied with confidence that victory was assured to the Christians. A few days previously the Saint had read these mysterious words on the altar where he was celebrating the Holy Sacrifice: 'Fear not, John, but continue valiantly as thou hast begun, because in virtue of My Name and of the holy Cross, thou shalt obtain a victory over the Turks.'

The meaning of this promise addressed to St. John personally was manifested on the morrow. The poor and undisciplined men, of whom Hunyad had complained, were put to combat with one hundred and fifty thousand fierce Mahometans, perhaps as good soldiers as the world has ever seen, because the sense of fighting for religion and country infused a double vigour into their arms. Already the standard of the Prophet waved over Belgrade, when John, lifting his crucifix ardently repeated, 'Jesus! Jesus!' The Christians roused themselves to a desperate effort. Hunyad executed a charge so furious that the Turks fell back, startled from their presumption to an excessive panic. That Holy Name of Jesus coming from the lips of a Saint was a miraculous war-cry: when the Christians repeated it after St. John, it seemed as if the whole atmosphere echoed back the invincible Name. The Turks, who had almost begun to conquer, now gave way in disorder and fled, yet not before they had left the flower of their magnificent host and their war chariots behind them in face of the demolished fortifications. Mahomet himself barely escaped with his life. It was the 22nd of July, 1456: God had saved Christendom at the prayer of His servant. 'Let your Holiness rejoice in God,' wrote the Saint to Callistus from the still smoking battle-field, 'and offer Him praise, glory, and honour, for He alone has done wonderful things. Neither I, poor and useless servant, nor the inexperienced Crusaders, the children of your Holiness, could have effected this by our own strength. The Lord God of armies has done all: to Him be glory throughout all ages. I write this in a hurry, returning wearied from the fight. I will soon send more particulars. From Belgrade, on the feast of St. Mary Magdalen, the day of victory.'

The two heroes had completed their course.

John Corvin Hunyad expired on the nth of August following, and the same Saint who had rallied the soldiers to the watchword of the Holy Name, soothed his passage into eternity. Then, his task over, the fiery old man's spirit could no longer resist the reaction of extraordinary fatigue and exertion. The material fight had had no terrors for him, and he could bear with patient joyfulness the last conflict between the soul and body. He was taken to the convent at Wilak, which had belonged to the Conventuals, but which the Saint with his practical mind, wished to secure to the Observance, and effectually did do so by dying in it. His mortal sickness began on the 6th of August; at first he did not recognize the fact that his martyrdom of desire was at hand, namely, that God called him to die not far from the battlefield, bearing about him the laurels of an earthly victory which was to be lengthened into eternity. 'I am not sure whether I shall die of this illness,' he said, 'but such a day (naming one) I will tell you.' And when the day came, having received a supernatural intimation that God was calling him away, he persevered in great constancy and cheerfulness until the end. Like Bernardine, he breathed forth his soul, stretched on the floor, his head upon the breast of one of his fellow-labourers, Father Jerome de Utino, his spirit fixed on God. If there was a thought for what he left on earth, that thought belonged to the Observance. John had passed just forty years in the army of St. Francis, from the 4th of October, 1416, till the 23rd of October, 1456, the day of his death. He was in his seventy-first year.

In the designs of God he was to succeed to Bernardine's apostolate, to oppose the Turks not so-much by arms as by purity and faith, and to become the precursor of the age of Ignatius. In all these things he had been faithful: it only remained to him to receive the crown.

Belgrade was to another and a greater victory like the morning star which ushers in perfect day. A hundred years later, in 1571, not John, but Pius stood over the fight, and Christendom was saved forever from the danger of a Turkish invasion. 'The night before the battle of Lepanto, and the day itself, aged as he was, and broken with disease, the Saint had passed in the Vatican in fasting and prayer. All through the Holy City the monasteries and the colleges were in prayer too. As the evening advanced, the Pontifical treasurer asked an audience of the Sovereign Pontiff on an important matter, Pius was in his bedroom, and began to converse with him; when suddenly he stopped the conversation, left him, threw open the window and gazed up into Heaven. Then closing it again, he looked gravely at his official, and said: 'This is no time for business; go, return thanks to the Lord God. In this very hour our fleet has engaged the Turkish, and is victorious.' As the treasurer went out, he saw him fall on his knees before the altar in thankfulness and joy.[189]

---

[189] *The Turks* p. 191.

CHAPTER XIV.

Actions not Words.

The martyrs fill up "what is wanting of the suffering of our Lord:" apostles and wonder-workers carry on the work of His Ministry. The lives of St. Vincent, St. Bernardine, and St. John Capistran were like pages of the Gospel enacted before the world. The sick, the blind, the deaf and dumb had only to ask for health to receive it; and miraculous power in these Saints was so great that it seemed only natural to petition them for gifts, which are of themselves beyond the province of man. The very formulas which they used are full of evangelical simplicity and strength, and they bear a strong family likeness to those of our Lord. 'Go in peace, thy faith hath made thee whole.' 'If thou canst believe, all things are possible to him that believeth.' Only three resurrections from the dead are recorded as worked by our Lord, yet St. John tells us that 'He did also many other things which if they were written every one, the world itself would not be able to contain the books that should be written.'[190]

The wonder-workers of His Church supply these blank pages, and the three saints in question reproduced in a particular and forcible manner the preaching of the Lord's Ministry. Our Lord gave three years out of His thirty-three to the active work of saving souls, passing thirty in humble submission to our Lady and St. Joseph. Obscurity and the religious novitiate answered in the lives of these

---

[190] St. John xx. 25.

disciples to Nazareth, but where their Master had spent three years, they devoted the flower of their life. Our Lord sketched the outline of the book which His followers were to fill with deeds and words so like His own that their parentage could not be a matter of doubt to any man.

The evils of the fifteenth century, which required so forcible an image of our Lord's Ministry for their correction may be summed up in the words of Holy Scripture: 'The beloved grew fat and kicked: he grew fat, and thick, and gross, he forsook God Who made him, and departed from God his Saviour.'[191] Worldliness had infected all orders of the State; in which condition of society the close relation between the civil and the spiritual powers, itself a great blessing, became instrumental to evil by allowing the existence of great corruption in spiritual places. The Schism of the West had moreover impaired the lawful authority of the Holy See. The times were out of joint. The remedy which our three saints strove to apply was uniform: it was the carrying out through the whole field of Christian action the warning: 'Repent, and do thy first works.'

From 1398 to 1456 a great movement of penance was carried on by them in the heart of Catholic life. The summons to preach it in a special way came to a Saint whose birth had been marked by supernatural occurrences. His life corresponded entirely with these heavenly prognostics, for it may be expressed in two words, purity and strength. Long years after Vincent had definitely fixed his path on earth in making choice of St. Dominic's

---

[191] Deut. xxxii. 15.

Order, he was one day musing with sadness upon the fittest remedy to oppose to the Schism. Then he beheld our Lord, Who came to answer his thought, and bade him 'preach His Gospel,' treating the nations of Europe as fallen, and in fact they had fallen into the worst kind of practical unbelief, which comes not of ignorance but of moral corruption. For the space of twenty years Vincent, like another John the Baptist, went from place to place crying out: 'Do penance, for the Kingdom of God is at hand.' There were no intervals of repose, his apostolate was in itself his rest, though a rest only appreciated by the saints. But that which is apt to strike other men in an apostle of penance would not be the mere action of preaching, and Vincent with his daily sermon would have achieved small things had not his own example spoken before his voice. The multitude who are fair judges in a question had said to themselves: 'If Father Vincent does penance himself we will listen to him.' Works speak more potently than words.[192] So effectually indeed did he possess the spirit of penance that it is difficult to find a single feature in his life which was not the exact contrary to what nature would crave for and desire. A daily discipline, a short and uncomfortable sleep, food barely sufficient to sustain life, no abiding place on earth, because, like our Lord, his temporary home was with the sinner, there where he could reap the most plentiful harvest for his Divine Master. The same feature is visible in Bernardine of Siena and John Capistran. Their personal austerity is marked; in the one case it accompanied great innocence, in the other it was first adopted in the maturity of life, when habits are

---

[192] 'Validior est operis quam oris vox.'

no longer acquired with the same facility. In our days hard work is too often apt to be considered the substitute of penance; these apostolical labourers might have alleged their daily toils, their weary wanderings after souls, but they knew too well the nature of the demon with whom they had to deal. He would not be driven out excepting by violence, and they remained friars to the end, keeping the austere Rule of St. Dominic and St. Francis even in the extremity of physical need.

When Bernardine promised his audience to show them the devil, and then pointed them out to each other, and when John told Nicholas V that immorality and riches stood in the way of his Order's spiritual progress, they show by their own words that they were fully aware of the moral dissoluteness of their day. Yet they did not meet the difficulty by waging war against vows so often broken, nor did they attack the Church, whose members at that time had in many cases fallen from their first fervour. The whole power of our Lord's ministry upon earth was directed to individuals; the Jewish people rejected Him, so did the Scribes and Pharisees. The servants followed in the footsteps of their Master. They preached penance, humility, and charity to individuals through the multitude. Our Lord searched out particular souls, amongst whom was an adulteress, whom He would not condemn; a Samaritan woman, whom He converted by the roadside; a blind man, who acknowledged Him to be the Son of God when others greater and better-gifted refused to accept Him. So Vincent Ferrer went to inns and country places, seeking souls whom he might, gain by personal influence, Bernardine worked his greatest miracles on the way, on a leper, for instance, who was banished from human society, and the Saint's simple gratitude for one night's hospitality called down the Divine blessing which was promised in return for one cup of cold water given in the Name of Jesus. In their obedience to the authority of the Church they were perfect. Wherever he went Vincent, although possessed of special faculties, craved the episcopal approbation. Bernardine, arraigned as a heretic, stood without a murmur before earth's highest tribunal, and John, at the simple wish of the Holy See, undertook extraordinary missions, against which he would not even allege his work for souls. Finally, in obedience to the same voice, John left his country for ever, sacrificing all strong ties of human affection, purified though it is in the heart of a Saint. In the lives of many churchmen immorality and love of riches were like clouds which seemed to be hiding the light of Catholic truth. Only one remedy could be successfully employed to bring about as perfect a day as is consistent with human frailty, the tears of contrition, which would dissolve the clouds in showers of penance. The Sacraments had fallen into disuse. These true sons of Holy Church set them up once more upon their pedestal. Every day Vincent Ferrer confessed his sins before beginning his ministry, as if to render himself worthier to become the confessor of sinners, and one of the duties he specially inculcated upon his bands of followers was the weekly reception of Penance and the Holy Eucharist. In Italy, too, the multitude had lost all relish for these two sacraments, which Bernardine and John constantly preached. The Apostle of Italy closed the door of the gambling houses by opening that of the tribunal of penance, and the Apostle of

Peace laid the foundation of a more lasting concord by openly proclaiming that its frequent use was by no means incompatible with the arduous life of a Christian soldier.

In the full measure of their several powers they glorified God. In His turn God glorified them, and through them that Catholic truth which their whole lives so entirely preached. Their miracles were counted by hundreds, and one day Vincent exclaimed in exhaustion, 'I have worked miracles enough to-day,' and transmitted his supernatural power to another. And John Capistran made use of a similar phrase when he once said, 'I am quite tired out, yet nothing has been done to-day; to-morrow you shall see the glory of God.' But, numerous as were the cures which they worked upon sick bodies, the wonders which they effected in the spiritual order carried off the palm of excellence. Our Lord promised that faith should have the power to move mountains. It is given to faith and charity to move cold hearts, mountains of the spiritual world, which bar the way of the soul.

Who does not see the point of an open and bloody persecution when it came in the first ages, to arouse Christians to a realization of their faith in their crucified Head? It is almost a commonplace that heresy in age after age has produced the drawing out and strengthening of the true doctrine. Even the great schism of the West — that most terrible chastisement — may have served in the end to quicken the sense of unity. The Turks, the sworn enemy of the Christian name, may have in God's designs acted the part of the hungry beasts of the amphitheatre and of the torturer's rack. They may have roused slumbering hearts to fight for their birthright of the faith. For there are times in history when the wheat becomes thin and meagre and the chaff abounds, and then an outward circumstance anticipates in some degree the separation of the last day. In His mercy Almighty God reduces the question to simple dimensions in order to render weak compromise impossible. When a Christian is brought to assert his faith before the altar of the idol, only two courses are open: he must confess or sacrifice.

The three Saints we have been describing were sent to avert one of these epochs, and they partially, and, it must be owned, only temporarily, succeeded. Instead of opposing the Papacy because of the schism, Vincent prepared a return to unity by his apostolate of penance; Bernardine, his successor, purified Italy from its sins in order that it might hold its natural place as the earthly home of the restored Papacy, and the preaching of John produced a respite from the Turks, which later enabled Christendom to gain the victory of Lepanto. Vincent Ferrer, Bernardine of Siena, and John Capistran, with their different watchwords, all had the same key-note, an intense love of souls, founded upon a yet more burning love of One Who is the Beginning and the End, the Resurrection and the Life.

These were reformers of the true stamp; they restored the fine gold to its brilliancy by cleansing the rust which had grown over it. Others afterwards usurped the name, who live now in history as destroyers, who tore down, but built not up. St. Vincent, St. Bernardine, and St. John

199

heralded the great movement accomplished by the Council of Trent and the saints who sprung up around it. It was sufficient glory for them to point out the way of a reformation which they might not complete, and to show forth in a corrupt generation, full of light, but wanting in love, the divine beauty of Catholic teaching, and the restorative power of penance.

4655367R00117

Printed in Germany
by Amazon Distribution
GmbH, Leipzig